GIRARD

A CANAL TOWN HISTORY

Members of the rural freight delivery pose for a photo outside of the North Girard Station. (Photo courtesy of West County Historical Association's Hazel Kibler Memorial Museum and Community House.)

THE MAKING OF AMERICA

GIRARD
A CANAL TOWN HISTORY

GEOFFREY L. DOMOWICZ

ARCADIA

Published by Arcadia Publishing,
an imprint of Tempus Publishing, Inc.
Charleston SC, Chicago, Portsmouth NH, San Francisco

Printed in Great Britain.

Library of Congress Catalog Card Number: 2003111657

For all general information contact Arcadia Publishing at:
Telephone 843-853-2070
Fax 843-853-0044
E-Mail sales@arcadiapublishing.com
For customer service and orders:
Toll-Free 1-888-313-2665

Visit us on the Internet at http://www.arcadiapublishing.com

CONTENTS

ACKNOWLEDGMENTS

In writing this text, it was not the author's intention to produce a definitive work detailing the history of every family that lived in Girard, Pennsylvania, for a work of that magnitude would not fit into the pages allotted here. Rather it was his intention to give the reader a good basic understanding of how the town of Girard developed over the course of history.

The author would like to thank the following individuals and organizations for their support and efforts in producing this text: the Erie County Historical Society, the West County Historical Association, the Hazel Kibler Memorial Museum and Community House, Stephanie Wincik, Steve Hudson, Carolyn Veith, and my beloved and supportive wife, Jennifer Domowicz.

INTRODUCTION

Girard, Pennsylvania, population 5,133, is located on the southern shore of Lake Erie. The borough took its name from Stephen Girard, a Philadelphia philanthropist who owned land in the area. The citizens in the area had hoped to entice him to invest in their community, but his early death brought an end to those hopes and the residents prospered on their own.

The community that eventually became known as Girard originally settled a little further west in the valley along Elk Creek at the first ridge (U.S. Route 20). With the coming of the Erie Extension Canal, the residents realized they would be too far west to benefit and moved their businesses up the hill and further east. Joseph Wells, one of the landowners in the new location, donated an area in the center of the planned community for a park.

The canal not only carried inexpensive fuel and other goods to and from Pittsburgh and Erie, it also brought Dan Rice, a famous clown and circus owner of the day. He liked the borough enough to settle there in 1854 and at the end of each touring season would arrive with his entourage and animals, to the disturbance and annoyance of many of the more conservative residents. At the end of the Civil War, Rice arranged to erect a monument to honor the officers and soldiers from Erie County, the first in the United States for this purpose. Today that monument still stands in the middle of Main Street (Route 20) next to Wells Park and is the focal point of the annual Memorial Day observance and the community's Dan Rice Days each August.

Four of the community's prominent leaders for many decades were the Battles, the Webster, the McConnell, and the Kibler families. The

Battleses and Websters were related by marriage and united in business. Rush S. Battles, the most prominent, had business interests far beyond Girard. He established the R.S. Battles Bank on East Main Street, which survived until 1946 when it merged with the Girard National Bank and today is part of the National City Bank system. During the enforced bank holiday of 1933, his daughter Charlotte Elizabeth insisted the Battles Bank remain open. She and her uncle, Charles F. Webster, who managed the bank, are purported to have telegrammed President Franklin D. Roosevelt with regard to the enforced closing: "We're minding our business, you do the same."

Another famous business in the borough was the Louis Marx Toy Company, which operated for 58 years in the community. During World War II it turned its expertise to manufacturing war materials.

Today the community is proud of its heritage. Several former buildings that belonged to the Battles family are designated as the Battles Museums of Rural Life. During the nineteenth century, the congregation of the Universalist Unitarian Church along with its minister, Reverend Shipman, were very active "conductors" in the Underground Railroad. Since Girard was in the path of the Underground Railroad, many individuals in the community, like Henry Teller and Elijah Drury, were known to offer shelter and comfort to those fleeing souls just prior to and during the Civil War.

The West County Historical Society also is an active presence in the community and has its headquarters in the Hazel Kibler home on East Main Street. The society shares its building with the Elk Valley Model Railroad Club.

Girard, once known as a "show town" because of the number of circuses that wintered there, could now be called a "sports town." High school football and boys' and girls' basketball take priority with the townspeople during the fall and early winter. Over the years these teams have had many winning seasons and state championships.

The Erie Extension Canal has long been closed, but much of Main Street still appears as it was when Girard was the leading business and cultural center of West Erie County. The community is involved in an ongoing restoration and revitalization program, assisted by the Girard–Lake City Chamber of Commerce. Main Street's businesses are still housed in the old business blocks and fine homes. The town's period street lights, the town clock, and tree-lined streets give visitors the feeling of yesterday, but with today's convenience.

Chapter One

THE EARLY SETTLERS
1750–1832

When Northwestern Pennsylvania was first discovered by the Europeans, it, like the rest of the continent, was inhabited by various groups of Native Americans belonging to the Iroquois Nation. The people were of Mongoloid ancestry and completely unaware of European culture. The predominant group, an Iroquoian-speaking tribe known as the Eriez, lived along the south shore of Lake Erie from Toledo to Buffalo. They made their homes at the confluence of two streams or where these streams met with the lake within 5 miles of the lakeshore. They were horticulturists, hunters, and gathers who subsisted primarily on maize, beans, squash, berries of all kinds, and game animals. They were defeated and dispersed by the Seneca Nation, one of the tribes of the Iroquois Confederacy in 1656. Any survivors were adopted into the Seneca Nation as blood kinsmen, ending the existence of the Eriez Nation.

The information we have about the Eriez Indians does not come from original sources. Rather it comes from the diaries and communications of the French explorers and missionaries who did not enter this region until well after the defeat of the Eriez Indians. They learned about the "people of the cat nation" from rival tribes, the Hurons, the Neutrals, and the Senecas.

Extensive research has been conducted by Charles Kolb on the Eriez Indians. In his articles, he states that the Eriez people referred to themselves by several names, depending upon to whom they were speaking. Just like in our language today, we often refer to ourselves using our proper names, Christian names, nicknames, or aliases, depending upon the situation. As a result, the translation of their language has been difficult. A word that had previously been thought to mean "cat" is now thought by Dr. Kolb and other scholars to mean "raccoon." It is no wonder we know so little about them.

However, looking at a map, it is not difficult to determine why the Eriez Indians along with the early Europeans chose to settle in this region. Its proximity to the lakefront and the natural access to its waters created by Elk Creek were just part of the allure to settle in this region. Prior to 1788, the northern and western borders of Pennsylvania met in the lake 4 miles west of the peninsula, leaving the commonwealth with only 6 miles of lakeshore. Due to the terrain, access to the lake was restricted to the mouths of Elk and Walnut Creeks. From 1788 to 1792, state officials negotiated with the federal government to purchase the peninsula and adjacent lands to take advantage of the natural harbor it provided. In 1797, the Erie Triangle was purchased, giving the commonwealth an additional 24 miles of lakefront.

The first settlers within the limits of Girard Township were William Silverthorn and his son, Captain Abraham Silverthorn, who came in 1798 from Fayette County. The Silverthorns and those who followed settled along the banks of Elk Creek and established a little community known as Elk Creek Settlement. They utilized the water to run mills and transport goods from neighboring communities.

About 1799, Robert Brown, of Northumberland County, settled at the mouth of Elk Creek, but in 1804 he moved to Weigleville and from there to Erie. He was the father of William A. Brown and Mrs. George A. Eliot, of Erie City. These parties were followed in 1800 by Robert Porter, Isaac Miller, and John Kelley. Kelley, who was from Mifflin County, eventually moved to West Mill Creek in 1802 and died there the following year. In 1801, Jacob Coffman came from Somerset County, and located on the future site of Lockport; and about the same time Patrick Ward settled on the lake road, current day Route 5. Coffman, who was from Somerset County, Pennsylvania, was accompanied by his four sons. Conrad, one of the boys, went back to Somerset County around 1814, married there, and did not return to Girard until 1836, when his son J.C. was a young man of 17.

William and Samuel McClelland and William Crane, natives of Ireland, took up lands in the northeast part of the township in 1802. John Miller, from Fayette County, and George Kelley, from Mifflin County, settled in 1803. Joel Bradish and his two brothers, from Saratoga County, New York, and James Blair, from Fayette County, Pennsylvania, settled in 1804. Martin Taylor, from Chautauqua County, New York settled in 1813; William Webber, from Genesee County, New York in 1814; and Cornelius Haggerty in 1815.

In the year 1814, at the close of the war with Great Britain, the site of Girard Borough was partly included in the farm of John Taylor, whose log house was the only building there. At a later date, this land was owned by Daniel Sayre Sr., who purchased it from Taylor. Sayre sold it to Joseph Wells, who erected the first frame building within the borough limits.

The first mill on Elk Creek, within Girard Township, was built at West Girard in 1814 by Peter Wolverton and was owned successively by Dr. Rufus A. Hills; James C. Marshall and his brother-in-law, Addison Weatherbee; George Rowley; L.S. Wright; Loomis & Horton; and W.C. Culbertson. Dr. Hills was the first physician to settle here in 1827, and since there was little need of his services, he occupied his time by managing the mill and eventually moved to Pittsburgh in 1830. James C. Marshall, an Erie attorney, along with his brother-in-law, Addison Weatherbee, operated not only the mill, but also the distillery and the general store until Weatherbee's death in 1832, at which point Marshall disposed of his interests and devoted his entire time to the practice of his profession. In 1837, he was appointed the first postmaster of Girard. During Rowley's term, the mill burned down and was rebuilt.

In 1816, Samuel Jenner and his son Peach, from Vermont; Justus Osborn and his son Philip, from Fredonia, New York; Abner Boder, from Connecticut; and Scott Keith and his wife, from Pittsford, Vermont; all settled here. In later years, settlers included: Elijah Drury from Genesee

County, New York, in 1817; Thomas Stewart, Ethan Loveridge, and Nathan Sherman from Oneida County, New York in 1818; Asa Battles Sr. from Chautauqua County, New York, in 1822; and Joseph Long from Massachusetts, in 1825; Matthew Anderson from Chenango County, New York, in 1830; George Traut from Columbia County, New York, in 1831; James Miles from Union Township, Pennsylvania; Titus Pettibone from Wyoming County, New York, in 1832; and William Kirkland in early 1833. Among other early settlers, the date of whose arrival has not been ascertained, were Messrs. Taggart, Pickett, Badger, Martin, Wells, Clark, Laughlin, and Wolverton. The last four—Wells, Clark, Laughlin, and Wolverton—along with Battles, were the first who located within the current site of Girard Borough. Wells and Battles owned most of the land within the corporate limits.

Asa Battles Sr., a veteran of the War of 1812 originally from Dedham, Massachusetts, sold his farm in Chautauqua County, New York for $800 and moved to Fairview Township sometime in late 1822. The site where he settled was within the future borough limits of Girard. In early 1823, Battles purchased 95 acres and a partially finished house from Thomas Stewart for $1,130 east of Elk Creek Settlement on present day Myrtle Street. Stewart had settled in this region from Oneida County, New York in 1818. Battles finished constructing the house and returned to Chautauqua County for his wife and family.

In April of 1824, upon reaching his family in Chautauqua County, Battles found that his father had taken terminally ill. Upon his father's death, he sold off all the property and with the inheritance from his father's estate; he purchased an additional 240 acres in then Fairview Township. He moved his pregnant wife and four children to their new home east of Elk Creek Settlement and began life again.

The first formal school held in Girard Township was taught in what is now Girard Borough, by J. Swan in the year 1809 in his private residence. He was then in his sixteenth year. The following year Swan moved to Swan Ville and taught school in Mill Creek Township. A log schoolhouse was then built in Girard and stood in the southwestern part of the township, in which classes were taught in 1819 by Miles Bristol. This schoolhouse was destroyed by fire in 1823 and another erected in the same locality. About 1822, lessons were also being taught by Nancy Kelly in a frame building that stood on the Ridge Road at the foot of the Girard Hill. Another school was held in a private house, situated 1 mile east of Girard, around 1823, taught by Desdemona Fuller.

By 1827, the village school was held in the lower floor of a log building that stood a little to the rear of the Smith & Lowe drug store on Main Street, while the second floor of the building was used as the Masonic Lodge room. Tabitha Mashon was teaching about this time. Although records of exactly what was being learned in the schools by the children do not exist, it is generally believed that the lessons centered on the "three R's": reading, writing, and arithmetic.

Chapter Two

THE INCORPORATION OF A TOWN

1832–1848

In 1832, the township of Girard was carved out of the surrounding townships of Elk Creek, Fairview, and Springfield. The township took its name from Stephen B. Girard, a Philadelphia philanthropist who owned a large body of land in the adjoining township of Conneaut. Citizens in the yet-to-be-named township had hoped to entice him to invest in their community, but his early death brought an end to those hopes. Just before his death, however, Girard put up mills on his Conneaut property and made other improvements, which were expected to benefit the whole area.

Stephen B. Girard was born in Bordeaux, France. At the age of 24 he became captain and part owner of a ship engaged in the West Indian and American coastal trade. In 1776 he settled in Philadelphia and became a merchant. Two years later he resumed his trading activities with the West Indies, accumulating a sizable fortune. In 1810 he invested about $1 million in shares of the First Bank of the United States. In 1812, when the charter of the bank lapsed, he purchased a controlling interest in its stock and continued the business as the Bank of Stephen Girard. During the War of 1812 he was an important financial supporter of the U.S. government; and in 1814 he subscribed for 95 percent of the war loan of $5 million. When the Second Bank of the United States was chartered in 1816, Girard became one of its principal stockholders and was a dominant influence on its policy for many years.

The fortune that Girard left at his death was probably the largest in the United States up to that time, amounting to about $7.5 million; the bulk of which he designated for philanthropic purposes. His will, which made legal history, provided money for municipal improvements, especially the improvement of the Philadelphia police system and for the establishment of a school or college for "poor, white, male orphans." In the regulations for the management of the institution, the will provided that no minister or ecclesiastic of any sect might hold office in the school or enter upon its premises, and that no teaching of religious doctrine in a denominational sense should be permitted. The heirs at law contested the will in 1836, and in 1844 the statesman and orator Daniel Webster argued for the heirs before the U.S. Supreme Court, making a famous plea for Christianity, without prevailing.

Johnny K. Ward, the first white male born within the present limits of Girard, related the following version of how the township got its name:

> I remember that a petition was circulated for the creation of the new township and I was one of the signers. A meeting for the purpose of selecting a name for the new township was held in the spring of 1832 in what now is the borough of Girard. Andrew Jackson was president at the time, and several of those who attended the meeting were in favor of naming the new township after him. I was one of them. The chairman of the meeting asked the Jacksonites to arise, one at a time, and give his reason why he favored naming the proposed new township after the "General."
>
> I sprang to my feet and said I was in favor of Jackson because he was the son of an Irish emigrant. My father also came from Ireland, and naturally I was a Jacksonite because "Old Hickory" had whipped the British at New Orleans, which was the last battle in the war of 1812.
>
> Someone proposed calling the new township Girard, after the Philadelphia mariner, merchant and banker, who had died a short time before. He was lauded as a great man who had done much

to win the war as General Jackson. Quite an argument developed, in which everyone took part, and for a time it looked as if we were going to have a debate accompanied with fisticuffs.

I guess that I did more than my share of talking, and finally the matter was put to a vote. It resulted in overwhelming majority for those who favored Girard and Girard it was named. I still think it should have been called Jackson Township.

Bounded on the north by Lake Erie, on the east by Fairview and Franklin Townships, on the south by Conneaut and Elk Creek Townships, and on the west by Springfield Township; the Township of Girard at its widest part is 6-and-a-quarter miles from east to west by 7-and-three-eights from north to south. Southeast of Girard Borough, the remains of an ancient mound can still be seen today. This mound was one of a chain of four that extended in a southwesterly direction through East Springfield toward Conneaut Creek. These mounds were exactly alike, consisting of high, round earthwork enclosing a space of about three-fourths of an acre, with apertures at regular intervals. Similar ruins were also found in Conneaut, Harbor Creek, Wayne, and Concord Townships and are believed to be the remains of some ancient civilization.

The early residents of the area had established a small, thriving community located on the west bank of Elk Creek, a site of the Reed's Stage Company's extensive stables and changing places for their teams. According to the *Erie Weekly Gazette*, the stables were burned in 1832: "Fire on the night of January 7, destroyed two barns belonging to Joseph Wells in Fairview Township with all their contents. Fifteen horses, harness, grain, etc. were burned. The horses and harness were the property of the Reed line of stages." The small village also boasted a number of stores, four taverns, two tanneries, an oil mill, a distillery, and several smaller establishments. Unfortunately for the community, by late 1836, land surveyors from the Canal Company had entered the area acquiring land and surveying for the Erie Extension of the Pennsylvania Mainland Canal.

The Erie Extension would link the great city of Pittsburgh with Lake Erie, thus providing the Commonwealth of Pennsylvania with an interior transportation system linking the Port of Philadelphia with the Great Lakes System. Utilizing rivers and other natural waterways, along with portions of railroad and hand dug canals, goods originating in England and other parts of Europe could now be transported throughout the commonwealth and to many points west.

The mouth of Elk Creek figured extensively in the early plans of internal improvement, as well as in the courts of the county and state. When the canal was under discussion, there was a bitter strife as to the adoption of the eastern route by way of Waterford or the western one by way of Girard. The legislature, at length and upon the recommendation of the chief engineer in charge, adopted the western route. Next, a dispute as to whether the terminus of the canal should be at Erie or at the mouth of Elk Creek developed. In June of 1831, Governor Wolf, accompanied by state surveyors and members of the state legislature, visited the mouth of Elk Creek to "ascertain from personal observation the advantage, if any, for the formation of a harbor at this point." No action was taken. Eventually, the decision favored the former.

On March 3, 1837, pending the decision of the proper terminus, a contract was entered into between James Miles, of Girard; Thaddeus Stevens, then a member of Governor Andrew Rigner's "Kitchen Cabinet"; and Charles Ogle, a state Congressman. The three men were looking to build a city at the mouth of the creek. Miles was to sell 200 acres of land on both sides of the stream to Stevens and Ogle. For the grand sum of $5,000 to be paid on August 1 and $95,000 to be paid when the rest of the lots were sold, Stevens was to work for the adoption of this site as the terminus of the canal, and Ogle was to obtain an appropriation from Congress for the improvement of the harbor. The project failing, Miles sued Stevens and Ogle for the $5,000. The case was carried to the Supreme Court and decided in favor of the defendants.

Construction of the Erie Extension of the Pennsylvania Mainland Canal began on July 4, 1838 and by 1845, the canal was in full operation. Just as investors had hoped, business along the canal was profitable. Small towns and settlements sprang up almost overnight in an effort to partake in the potential profits from handling goods or entertaining travelers.

Thomas S. Woodcock, a New York engraver, described his seven-day trip on the Erie Canal between Pittsburgh and Lockport (presently known as Platea, a small community 5 miles south of Girard Township) in an 1842 letter. The following is an excerpt describing some of the struggles while traveling the canal:

> . . . These Boats have three Horses, go at a quicker rate, and have the preference in going through the locks, carry no freight, are built extremely light, and have quite Genteel Men for their Captains, and use silver plate. The distance between Pittsburg and Lockport is 80 Miles; the passage is $3.50, which includes board. There are other Boats called Line Boats that carry at a cheaper rate, being found for 2/3 of the price mentioned. They are larger Boats, carry freight, have only two horses, and consequently do not go as quickly and moreover have not so select a company. Some boats go as low as 1 cent per Mile, the passengers finding themselves.
>
> The Bridges on the Canal are very low, particularly the old ones. Indeed they are so low as to scarcely allow the baggage to clear, and in some cases actually rubbing against it. Every Bridge makes us bend double if seated on anything, and in many cases you have to lie on your back. The Man at the helm gives the word to the passengers: "Bridge," "very low Bridge," "the lowest in the Canal," as the case may be. Some serious accidents have happened for want of caution. A young English Woman met with her death a short time since, she having fallen asleep with her head upon a box, had her head crushed to pieces. Such things however do not often occur, and in general it affords amusement to the passengers who soon imitate the cry, and vary it with a

command, such as "All Jackson men bow down." After such commands we find few aristocrats.

Life along the banks of the Erie Extension Canal soon began to take on a feeling all of its own. Songwriters and story tellers began to romanticize about the ideal lifestyle of the people who lived and worked on its banks. One such song, "Low Bridge, Everybody Down" written in 1905 by Thomas S. Allen, summed up this sentiment, although actually written about a neighboring canal in New York State:

> I've got a mule, and her name is Sal, fifteen miles on the
>   Erie Canal.
> She's a good ol' worker an' a good ol' pal, fifteen miles on the
>   Erie Canal.
> We've hauled some barges in our day, filled with lumber, coal,
>   and hay,
> And we know every inch of the way from Albany to Buffalo.
>
> Low bridge, everybody down! Low bridge, for we're comin'
>   through a town!
> And you'll always know your neighbor; you'll always know your
>   pal, if you've ever navigated on the Erie Canal.
>
> We'd better look around for a job, ol' gal, fifteen miles on the
>   Erie Canal!
> 'Cause you bet your life I'd never part with Sal, fifteen miles on the
>   Erie Canal!
> Git up there, mule, here comes a lock, we'll make Rome 'bout six
>   o'clock, one more trip and back we'll go right back home to Buffalo.

Once the canal opened, many people firmly believed that if the community of Elk Creek was going to prosper from the canal in any way, it had to relocate to the top of the hill. Most business owners vacated their establishments along the banks of Elk Creek and built new shops and homes. Those that remained along Elk Creek were the mill owners, who depended upon the running waters of Elk Creek to operate their equipment. The new little community near the canal eventually became known as Girard Borough while the original Elk Creek Settlement became known as West Girard around the same time.

The first buildings in the new village on top of the hill were near the canal, and the first tavern occupied a site a little west of the current Methodist Episcopal Church. George Dougherty was one of the first businessmen to open his new freight hauling company within the village's limits. On May 23, 1836, he posted an advertisement in the *Erie Gazette* that stated:

> The subscriber will run Wagons constantly between this place and Pittsburg, during the present summer, on the Turnpike road, passing through Waterford, Cambridge, Meadville, Georgetown, Mercer, Centreville Butler, and Bakerstown. The distance is 128 miles. He keeps large and small covered Wagons, for carrying Freight and Baggage, in good order, and all freight intrusted to him will be transported without delay, and cheaper than it can be done from any port on the Lake. Carriage on freight from 75 cents to $1.00 per hundred pounds.

In 1846, the new village was incorporated as a borough and officially named Girard, Pennsylvania. Its first officers were: Burgess Mason Kellogg; Council Members John McClure Jr., Leffert Hart, H. McConnell, and George H. Cutler; and Clerk L.S. Jones.

Several significant buildings that were constructed during this period still exist in the town today. One of them is Hutchinson's house, located at 172 Main Street East. This Georgian style house was built by Judge Myron Hutchinson in 1830, making it the oldest house in Girard. Hutchinson served as justice of the peace, postmaster, and judge for Erie County. The

Keystone Block, 13–21 Main Street East, had its beginnings in 1832 and still remains as one of the oldest business blocks between Cleveland and Buffalo. This was the beginning of the Girard commercial district. Theodore Ryman opened his hat business on the eastern corner and later sold boots and shoes. James Webster's house, 209 Main Street East, was built around 1832, making it the second oldest house in the borough. James Webster came to Girard in 1827 and engaged in a thriving mercantile business with his brother-in-law, Henry McConnell. There were no more than 20 buildings in the little hamlet when the firm of Webster & McConnell was established. But the two men foresaw the possibilities of the town's growth.

With the only newspaper of the time the *Weekly Gazette*, owned by Joseph M. Sterrett of Erie, regular ads began to appear in the newspaper from the inception of the firm. Farmers who took the *Weekly Gazette* would travel 10–15 miles to do their trading at Webster & McConnell. One such ad reads: "Webster & McConnell, dealers in dry goods, groceries, crockery, stoneware, sole and upper leather, glass, hardware, nails, etc., which they are selling extremely low for cash or good credit. All those wishing to dispose of their grain or cash, on first rate terms, are requested to call and examine goods and prices."

The Plum Fish Business, 236 Main Street West, was constructed around 1845 by Walter Plum. The rear portion of this building was in the heart of the canal era's business district. Canal barges were drawn beside the building and loaded with grain for shipment to eastern markets. The front portion of the building was used as a fish monger's shop and sold the freshest days' catch from the lake and Elk Creek. James Nichols's house, 28 Myrtle Street, was built around 1846 by a person or persons unknown. The house was later owned by James Nichols from 1860 to 1870. Nichols made his earnings as a traveling salesman. John Gulliford Sr.'s house is located at 47 South Park Row. This grand brick replacement home was built around 1848 for John Gulliford Sr. Gulliford owned the local hardware business, which was established in 1839 on Main Street West.

Chapter Three

THE GREAT CANAL ERA
1848–1860

Down the eastern seaboard of the United States, the Appalachian Mountains present a barrier to most forms of commercial transportation, and this was especially true in the mid-1800s. The state of New York has a convenient passage in the Mohawk Valley through these mountains; Pennsylvania, however, has no such gateway to the western part of the state and beyond. In colonial days, to overcome the Appalachian barrier, traders drove trains of pack horses or mules up and down the mountain ridges. Each animal carried a load of approximately 200 pounds. Consequently, the cost of transporting goods over such heights was prohibitive of commerce on any extended scale. Nature herself, however, had provided a partial solution to the problem. The Delaware, Susquehanna, and Allegheny Rivers pierced the mountains, range after range, by way of gorges known locally as "water gaps"; and in the valleys between these ranges flowed countless navigable tributaries.

From the earliest days of Pennsylvania, plans were studied for encouraging trade by way of the various waterways throughout the commonwealth. Founder William Penn, as early as 1690, dreamed of connecting Delaware River traffic with the Susquehanna River. His thought was to build a canal to follow the upstream course of Tulpehocken Creek from its mouth on the Schuylkill River. The downstream course would follow the Swatara Creek to its mouth on the Susquehanna River. Such a canal would bind the Delaware, Schuylkill, and Susquehanna Rivers into one great system of transportation.

A century was to pass, however, before Pennsylvania had its first artificial waterway. In 1797 the Conewago Canal, built on the west bank of the

Susquehanna below York Haven to enable boats to avoid the rocks and rapids of the Conewago Falls, was declared operable by the state. Its purpose was to link river traffic safely with the town of Columbia and with the turnpike running from that town to Philadelphia.

The great spur to Pennsylvania canal building came from the example of the Erie Canal three decades later. As the New York state project went forward between 1817 and 1825, Pennsylvania stock companies improved navigation on the Schuylkill. The Union Canal Company in 1828 joined the Schuylkill with the Susquehanna by a canal along Tulpehocken and Swatara Creeks, connecting Middletown with Philadelphia by water.

Meanwhile, Pennsylvania citizens called for a system of public works that would provide access to Philadelphia for the timber, mining, and manufacturing in all parts of the Commonwealth, even those regions west of Allegheny Mountain. The Pennsylvania Assembly of 1824 gave authorization, and by 1834 the Pennsylvania Canal, which surmounted Allegheny Mountain by carrying canal boats, passengers, and cargoes on the Allegheny Portage Railroad between Hollidaysburg and Johnstown, was completed.

Other divisions of the state canal were advanced or completed by that same year. Publicly owned canals ascended along the Delaware from Bristol to Easton and along the two great branches of the Susquehanna to Lock Haven and Nanticoke. At the same time private projects had made the Lehigh and Schuylkill Rivers open for trade. By 1845 both private and public waterway connections had been established to link the cities of Pittsburgh, Meadville, and Erie by the Ohio River, the Beaver Division Canal, the Erie Extension, and the Franklin Line. Other waterway terminals within the Commonwealth connected with New Jersey canals on the east and Ohio canals on the west, furthering interstate commerce during the same period. A towpath bridge on the Susquehanna encouraged trade with Chesapeake Bay and Maryland by linking the Pennsylvania Canal at Columbia with the Susquehanna and Tidewater Canal at Wrightsville.

The building of the state-owned Pennsylvania canal system was a great and intricate feat in engineering. Channels had to be dug along difficult river banks and through mountain valleys high above sea level. Aqueducts had to be built to carry the canal across rivers and creeks. Allegheny Mountain had to be crossed. The great waterway required not only two subsidiary railroads but an elaborate system of lift locks, aqueducts, feeders, canal basins, wasteweirs, towing paths, bridges, and the like. Travel and transport were slow on canal boats drawn by mules or horses, with frequent passings through locks or transfer over the mountains by the levels and inclined planes of the Allegheny Portage Railroad. Four miles per hour for cargo boats was standard.

By an act of the legislature on April 11, 1825, Pennsylvania established the first official Board of Canal Commissioners for the Commonwealth. After a summer and autumn of surveys directed by the board in many parts of the state, a second act was passed on February 25, 1826. This act formally initiated a program of public canal and railroad works which was to revolutionize traffic and industry.

Fourteen years later, Pennsylvania's system of canals, including the 82-mile Columbia and Philadelphia Railroad and the 36-mile Allegheny Portage Railroad, totaled up to 726 miles of railways and waterways in operation, while another 208 miles were under construction.

The great heyday of the Pennsylvania canals lasted for hardly more than a quarter of a century. By the mid-1850s the corporate railroads of the state, with their ever increasing rapidity of transportation, had become vigorous and aggressive competitors, and the Commonwealth found it financially advisable to dispose of its canals to private railroad and canal companies. As early as 1843, the state sold the Erie Extension Canal, the French Creek Feeder, and the Franklin Line to private operators.

Rates of toll charged on the canal after March 15, 1845 drastically increased, just another factor that helped to bring about its eventual demise. According to the official Office of Erie Canal records, the following rates were enacted by Rufus Reed, president, on March 4, 1845:

The Great Canal Era: 1848–1860

I.—PROPERTY CHARGED WITH TOLL BY WEIGHT.

ONE AND A HALF MILLS PER 1000 LBS. PER MILE

Coal—mineral, Heading and hoop poles for barrels and hogsheads, Iron Ore, Salt, Staves for pipes, hogsheads and barrels

TWO MILLS PER 1000 LBS. PER MILE

Ashes—leached, pot and pearl, Cotton—raw, Coke, Gypsum, Iron—scrap, pig and broken castings, Lime and limestone, Lead—bar, pig, and shot, Manure, Stone—entirely unwrought, Sills—locust

THREE MILLS PER 1000 LBS. PER MILE

Anvils, Bacon, Beef—salted, Butter, Bricks, Burrs, (French) in blocks, Cheese, Clay—for ware, Coffee, Sugar, Molasses, Fish, Flour, Grindstones, Hay and Straw, Headings and belts for cedar ware, Hemp and hempen yarns, Lard and Lard Oil, Marble sawed or in block, Oats, Oils of all kinds (except Castor), Potatoes and other vegetables, Pork, Rails—split in boats or scows, Railroad Iron, Rosin and pitch, Staves—for cedar ware, Tallow, Tar, Tile, Tobacco—not manufactured, Window glass and glassware, Wool, Wheat

FOUR MILL PER 1000 LBS. PER MILE

Agricultural productions not particularly specified, Bark—ground, Barley, Barn and ship stuffs, Buckwheat, Charcoal, Corn (Indian), Cider, Earthenware, Hops, Iron—castings, blooms and anchonics, Rye, Slate for roofing, Stone wrought, Seeds of all kinds

FIVE MILLS PER 1000 LBS. PER MILE

Agricultural implements, carts, wagons, sleighs, ploughs and mechanics tools, Apples and other green fruit, Bales of brown muslin or sheeting, Beer, Porter and Ale, Copper, Feathers,

Hardware and Cutlery, Hides, Iron—bar, rolled, slit, hammered or sheet, Leather—dressed and undressed, Lead—white, Live stock, Mahogany wood, Millstones, Nails and spikes, Queensware and Chinaware, Rags, Steel steam engines and sugar mills, Skins—furs and peltry, Soapstone, Stoneware, Straw paper, binders board and slates, Tin and tinware, Tobacco—manufactured, Whiskey

EIGHT MILLS PER 1000 LBS. PER MILE
Dry goods, Drugs and medicines, Furniture—household, Groceries (except coffee, sugar and molasses), Lead—red and litharge, Liquors—foreign, Marble—manufactured, Oysters, Paints and dye stuffs except white lead, Paper—writing and printing, Ropes and cordage, Rails if conveyed on rafts, Specie or bullion, All articles not enumerated.

II.—ARTICLES CHARGED BY NUMBER OR MEASURE.
Bark unground—5 mill per cord; Boards, planks, scantling and all other sawed timber or stuff conveyed in boats or scows—3 mills per 1000 board feet measure or 1 mill if conveyed on rafts; Posts, for fencing, if carried in boats or scows—4 mills per 100 or 8 mills if conveyed on rafts; Shingles, long—2 mills per 1000; Shingles, short—1 mill per 1000; Timber, round or square, if conveyed in boats or scows—3 mill per 100 cubic feet or 1 mill if conveyed on rafts; Wood for fuel, if conveyed in boats or scows—4 mills per cord or 1 mill if conveyed on rafts

III.—TOLL ON BOATS.
Boat towed by three or more horses, designed exclusively for passengers—4 cents per mile; Boat towed by two horses designed exclusively for passengers—3 cents per mile; Freight and packet boat—2 cents per mile; Boat carrying freight only—2 cents per mile

IV.—TOLL ON PASSENGERS—ON EACH PERSON OVER TWELVE YEARS OF AGE.

If transported on boats towed by three or more horses, designed exclusively for passengers—4 cents per mile; If transported on boats towed by two horses, designed exclusively for passengers—3 cents per mile; If transported on boats carrying freight and passengers—2 cents per mile; On extra baggage (over 50 lbs per passenger)—8 cents per mile per 1000 lbs.

If two or more articles chargeable with different rates of toll shall be contained in the same cask, box, or thing, the whole shall be charged with the highest rate chargeable on any article so contained.

Every float lying in or occupying any public basin connected with canal, except while receiving or discharging cargo (for which purpose forty-eight hours are allowed if necessary) shall be charged twenty-five cents a day for each and every day.

V.—TOLL AT OUTLET LIFT LOCKS OR BRIDGEWATERS.

Every loaded ark, Durham, river boat, or other craft built expressly for navigating the canal, passing through the locks—25 cents each; Empty—18 cents each.

These new rates made traveling the canal more expensive than ever before. The same seven day, 80-mile trip on a three horse boat from Pittsburgh to Lockport that cost Thomas S. Woodcock $3.50 in 1842, three years later would cost him considerably more. As a matter of fact, the basic trip would cost $3.20 plus a portion of the additional fees attached to the boat on which he was traveling. These additional fees; the toll on the boat, $3.20; the per day use fee, $1.75; and the 27 lock tolls, $6.75; totaling $11.70, now needed to be absorbed by the 16 passengers on average who usually traveled on each boat in order for the captain just to cover his expenses. This adds an additional 73¢ to the basic cost of $3.20; totaling

$3.93 that the captain must charge each passenger in order to cover his expenses, not to mention his profit margin. Consequently, the direct result of the new fee structure was that less passengers and freight could afford to travel in this manner.

The first company to lay its railroad tracks trough Girard Township was the Franklin Canal Company, which ran from the Ohio-Pennsylvania state line to Erie and was an extension of the Cleveland, Painesville and Ashtabula, which ran from Cleveland to the state line. The charter was granted in 1844 and supplemented in 1849 when construction began.

Meanwhile, work had already begun on a line east of Erie to the New York state line. This road, known as the Erie & North East, connected with the Buffalo & State Line Railroad into Buffalo. By November 17, 1852, both the Erie and North East railway lines, originating in Erie and traveling to all points east, and the Cleveland, Painesville & Ashtabula line serving all points west of Erie, were in operation. "November 20, 1852—On Wednesday last at about half past three the last spike was driven in the iron bands connecting New York City with Cincinnati," reported the Erie Observer. "A grand celebration in honor of the event will take place in this city on Tuesday next."

The first station was erected in 1851 by the Cleveland, Painesville & Ashtabula line to serve the residents of the Girard area. The station was built north of the town and named North Girard Station. The citizens of the town could now board one of 22 luxury trains that stopped at the new station to travel to Erie or Cleveland for business or pleasure.

Although travel was now available to Buffalo, passengers and freight had to disembark at Erie's Union Station to switch railway lines. The Erie and North East lines operated at a 6-foot gauge while the Cleveland, Painesville & Ashtabula line operated at a 4-foot-10-inch gauge. Because of the difference, Erie's Union Station became a major transportation hub. The attempt to standardize the railway gauge in late 1852 led to the Railroad Gauge War. Those associated with the railroad industry were infuriated with this proposal and actually tore up the newly laid 56-and-one-half inch "standard gauge" tracks. Eventually the courts became involved, issuing an order in 1853 that "all men were forbidden to tear up the railroad tracks." However, this did not have the effect that was intended. Women, or men dressed in women's clothes, took up where the men left off. Another court ruling later that year corrected the oversight by specifying that "any person or persons" caught tearing up the tracks would be severely punished.

By 1850 the population of Girard Township had grown to 2,443, inclusive of the communities of West Girard and North Girard, while the U.S. census gave Girard Borough a population of 400. The main thoroughfares of Girard Township were Lake Road and Ridge Road, both running to Erie; the two roads between North Girard and the borough (Rice Avenue and Lake Street), Meadville Road (also known as Route 18 today) through Lockport (Platea) and Cranesville to Meadville, and the Lexington Road into Conneaut Township. Ridge and Lake Roads were heavily settled and Ridge Road was unquestionably the finest in the county, having a fine row of shade trees on both sides almost the entire distance from Girard to Fairview. After the opening of the railroad in 1852, few persons cared to travel by coach, and the state-operated stage line was soon abandoned.

By 1853 the new Lake Shore Railroad traversed the whole township from east to west, crossing Elk Creek a short distance west of North Girard. The old wooden viaduct over this stream, built in 1852, was 115 feet high and 1,400 feet long. It was replaced in 1858 with a splendid culvert and extensive filling after it collapsed. The Erie & Pittsburgh Railroad intersected the Lake Shore almost a mile west of North Girard and ran southward across the township, parallel to and not far from the Springfield line. The New York, Chicago & St. Louis Railroad traversed the entire width of the township from east to west, crossing the Elk Creek Valley by a splendid iron bridge, within sight of Girard Borough. Its station was between the Borough of Girard and North Girard, on present day Nickel Plate Road.

GIRARD

A railroad of another kind was very active in Girard from 1840 to 1865, the Underground Railroad. Although not an actual physical railroad, this movement's purpose was to aid in the escape of fugitive slaves. Individuals from the area known to have participated in the Underground Railroad were Reverend Charles L. Shipman, Henry Teller, and Elijah Drury. Drury sheltered slaves in one of his barns along Elk Creek, while Teller openly escorted escaping slaves around the borough to buy supplies. Reverend Shipman, who lived in Andover, Ohio, moved to a house located at 121 Myrtle Street within the borough limits to become the minister of the Universalist Church. The house was built sometime before 1855 by a person unknown. Today, one of the graves in the old Drury family cemetery, located on Drury Road, is reported by the family's oral history to be that of a tortured runaway slave who died on the property.

In an interview conducted in February of 1938, Miss Effie Shipman, the daughter of Reverend Shipman, recalled her time in Girard:

> When I was about seven years old, my father, Reverend C.L. Shipman, removed from Andover, Ohio, to Girard. We lived for a short time in a tenant house on the Drury farm before going to a house on Myrtle Street, where we remained for nearly seven years. My father often told me that Mr. Drury kept runaway slaves in a secluded spot near Elk Creek until they were passed on to Erie and from there to Canada. I don't know this of my own personal knowledge, but I have no doubt of its truth. Mr. Drury was a man whose heart was filled with the milk of human kindness.

While the Erie Extension Canal was in operation, the residents of Girard prospered. The first boat was pulled through Girard in December of 1844 loaded with iron ore and coal from the Pittsburgh mines destined for ships in Erie harbor. By the time the town incorporated, Girard boasted 16 businesses, including hotels, harness shops, hardware stores, general stores, lawyers, doctors, dentists, lightning rod manufacturers, cobblers, theatres, an opera house, and numerous taverns. In fact, during the days of stage coaching on the Ridge Road, Girard was famous for its taverns, there having been no less than eight within 2 miles.

The Girard Academy was built by subscription in 1850 and opened in 1851 with 150 pupils. It had a students' boarding house attached, and for a while it was very successful. The first newspaper was the *Girard Free Press*, started about 1845 by S.D. Carpenter, who took Horace Greeley's advice, went west, became a prominent politician, and published a book at the commencement of the war, which furnished the texts for numberless Democratic editorials. The *Express*, the successor to the *Girard Free Press*, was purchased by T.C. Wheeler and William S. Finch on November 7, 1854, and the name was changed again to the *Republican*. It bore the motto, "Independent on all subjects, rabid on none." In 1855, Samuel Perley, working for the *Erie Gazette*, moved to Girard from Erie and merged the material in his city office with that of the *Republican*. Perley conducted this paper for several years.

The Erie Extension Canal first brought Dan Rice, the originator of the "Uncle Sam" persona, to the community in 1854. The town had its factions and those who did not like Rice and his socially unacceptable occupation did not like having the prankster as a resident. The adoption of Girard as the residence of Dan Rice had the further effect of drawing other caterers to public amusement there, and in course of time it became known far and wide as a "show town." Among the famous showmen who made their residence in Girard were Dr. James L. Thayer, who started as an employee of Dan Rice's; Charles W. Noyes, one of his pupils; Abe Henderson, Agrippa Martin, and Seymour Pease; all at one period were owners or part owners of extensive circuses. No less than five shows had been organized in the borough by 1860: Dan Rice's, Thayer & Noyes's, Rice & Forepaugh's, Anderson & Company's, and G.R. Spalding & Company's.

The public square of Girard was a gift from Joseph Wells, one of the first owners of the land, when the village was laid out. It was surrounded by a number of fine buildings, but its principal object of interest at that time was the Dan Rice residence, which occupied, with grounds, a full block on the north side. The Dan Rice property embraced 2.5 acres, enclosed on three sides by a heavy brick wall and ornamented with statuary, walks, arbors, and the choicest of trees, shrubbery, and flowers. The mansion itself was a large frame building. Within the enclosure were a fine conservatory and a brick barn costing $26,000. The cost of the wall around the grounds was $3,000. Dan Rice's first land purchase in Girard was in 1853, when he bought a small piece of land with a building on the northwest side of the square from Colonel John McClure for $18,000. In 1856 he moved there, and from that date Rice continued to add to his purchase until he had possession of the entire square, at a total cost of about $60,000.

The first bank organized in Girard was in 1859, under the firm name of Battles & Webster House of Banking by Rush S. Battles and Henry Webster. The two prominent businessmen of Girard served the residents until 1946 when they voluntarily merged with the other bank in town to form the Girard Battles National Bank.

Two years earlier, in April of 1857, Rush S. Battles began construction on an elaborate Italianate house on the ridge south of the town as his new personal residence for himself and his family. The 24-year-old graduate of the National Law School in Poughkeepsie, New York hired William Blackford of Erie to draw up the plans of the house in "the style and elevation to represent the same style for cornice, verandah, brackets, and observatory as used on the house owned by Moses Koch of Erie." Battles contracted Erastus Slater of Girard to build the house for himself, his mother, and his sisters for the sum of $550 cash, 1 acre of land, and room and board for Slater and his crew. The house was completed one year later and the family moved in during April of 1858.

As the town began to grow in numbers, various churches were formed based upon the different religious sects and upbringing of the citizens. Formalized religion became a part of the inhabitants of the area. One of the first churches of the township of Girard was the Methodist Episcopal, located at Fair Haven, on the Lexington road, in the southwest part of the township. The congregation was organized originally on January 7, 1815, at the house of William Webber, and reorganized by Reverend A. Hall in 1860. Their building was erected in 1861 at a cost of $3,000. Prior to its attachment to the Lockport Circuit, this congregation was a part of the circuit affiliated with the church at Girard. Another congregation of the same denomination was at Fairplain, upon the farm of C. Ziesenheim on Lake Road, organized in 1840 by Reverend J.H. Whallon, its first pastor. Its building was erected in 1841 at a cost of $800. Until 1880, this congregation was served by the pastors from Girard. It is presently connected with Fairview Circuit.

The churches of the Girard Borough were Presbyterian, Methodist Episcopal, Catholic, and Universalist Churches. The Methodist church, which had few superiors in the county for beauty of architecture and elegance of finish, was erected in 1868 at a cost of $30,000. However, the congregation was organized in 1815, by Reverend Ira Eddy, its first pastor, and built its first edifice in 1828. For many years the appointment was a portion of the Springfield Circuit.

St. John's Catholic congregation was organized about the year 1858 and soon thereafter put up a church building. The congregation was attended by visiting priests for a number of years. The Universalist society was organized in 1848 and in 1852 erected the building on Myrtle Street. This building later burned and the present structure was erected in 1867. Their pastors until 1860 were Reverend S.P. Carrolton preceded by Reverends E. Wood and C.B. Lombard.

The Presbyterian Church is a substantial brick building erected in 1835 on the corner of Main Street and Church Street, to which an old graveyard was attached. Its congregation was organized May 16, 1835, by Reverend Pierce Chamberlain and the first elders were Robert Porter and Philip Bristol. It was at first supplied by Reverend Edison Hart, who was stationed at Springfield.

The secret societies of the borough at the time were the Masonic Blue Lodge and Chapter and two lodges of the United Workmen. A Grange flourished for awhile, but had been disbanded by 1858. The Exodus Lodge, I.O. of G.T., was in existence in 1855; the Girard Lyceum was founded in 1855; a Young Men's Literary Association in 1859; and the Girard Guards, with D.W. Hutchinson as captain, were organized in 1860. The Union Agricultural Society of Girard was instituted as an auxiliary to the county society on July 25, 1856 and had a fair that year, and it continued to give annual exhibitions until the war began.

Some of the town's other historic buildings from this period included Dr. Benjamin C. Ely's house at 232 Main Street East, which was constructed in 1854 when Dr. Benjamin C. Ely moved to Girard from the McKean area. Ira and Susan Carpenter's house, located at 318 Main Street East, may have already existed in 1855 when Ira and Susan Carpenter moved in. In 1856, the elders of the Presbyterian Church purchased the Greek revival house and barn for use as their parsonage. Homer Hart's house, 404 Main Street East, is a fine example of a Greek revival home. Homer Hart, a retail merchant, had this house built around 1854 after purchasing the land from Myron Hutchinson. George Wright's house at 141 Myrtle Street was built by George Wright between 1854 and 1855 in the Greek revival style. The house was enlarged in 1883 by George Kibler.

Chapter Four

THE CIVIL WAR ERA

1860–1868

It was commonly remarked during the 1860s that the land between Walnut Creek, in Fairview and Crooked Creek, in Springfield, was the best along Lake Erie; and Girard Township was claimed by its citizens to be the choicest section. The lake plain was from 3 to 4 miles wide, a succession of steps that gave a pleasing variety to the country. Near the lake the soil was sandy, but on the ridge it became gravelly and was very productive. South of Girard Borough, the land continued to rise, and, except along Elk and Crooked Creeks, where there were some fine valley farms, the land was better adapted for grazing than grain. The whole township was a splendid fruit country, and many acres had been planted in grapes and strawberries. The strawberry crop was to Girard what the grape crop was and is to North East, Pennsylvania, vast quantities being raised annually and shipped to all points of the compass. The farm improvements averaged better than any other part of the lake shore, and the taste shown in some instances would be creditable to any locality. Land was valued at from $100 to $125 per acre along Ridge Road, from $60 to $100 along Lake Road, and from $35 to $60 in the south part of the township.

The only post office at the time was at the Girard Station located in North Girard, and the total population was 2,453 in 1860. The average person made their living on the area farms and markets and did not comment very often on the current changing politics of the day. Both pro-slavers and abolitionists occupied the township.

The Girard Cemetery is considered one of the handsomest burial grounds in the county and consists of a tract of 10 acres, neatly enclosed, laid out in walks, and containing many costly monuments. The Cemetery Association was charged in March of 1861, and the property was laid out the same year.

In 1860, Dan Rice, a father of two teenaged daughters, divorced his wife and became interested in the young daughter of a socially prominent family in town, Charlotte Rebecca McConnell. Her father, Henry McConnell, operated the largest mercantile business in the area along with his brother-in-law, James Webster, for more than 30 years. Given the sentiment of the townspeople towards Dan Rice, many were appalled at the showman's recent behavior.

The news of Dan Rice's marriage to Charlotte Rebecca McConnell on her eighteenth birthday, Monday, November 4, 1861, gained national attention. The *Cleveland Plain Dealer* reported that the bride was "a beautiful and accomplished lady and the only child of one of the wealthiest families of Girard. It is emphatically a 'love match,' both being most devoted." In her diary, Charlotte Webster Battles, Charlotte Rebecca McConnell's first cousin, wrote of the event: "Monday. Cold and windy. Mother, Ellen and I working at our house all day and evening. Water in the cellar. Rebecca went to Mrs. H's house and married Dan Rice. How can it be that she has ruined herself and broken her parent's hearts?"

On April 12, 1861 at 4:30 a.m., Union forces under the command of Major Anderson garrisoned at Fort Sumter, South Carolina were bombarded by Major P.T.G. Beauregard's Confederate Artillery. The American Civil War had begun. On April 15, 1861, President Lincoln called for 15 regiments to be formed from Pennsylvania, each consisting of 30 line officers and 1,300 men. Pennsylvanians answered that call by supplying the President with 25 regiments. The patriotic fervor within the commonwealth's borders was so high that the draft was not needed until October of the following year. Exempted were men over 45, the physically disabled, ministers, teachers, and school directors. By the time Pennsylvania's second draft was held, every able-bodied man between 20 and 45 was eligible.

The Civil War Era: 1860–1868

The citizens of Girard were quick to show their allegiance to the Union. The first war meeting in the county was held here on April 26, 11 days after the President's call for volunteers, and it was largely attended. Among those who made stirring speeches was George H. Cutler, a leading member of the legal bar.

Before May 1, Colonel John W. McLane's Erie regiment was not fully enlisted. Company G of that regiment was recruited from Girard, the company being organized the previous year as the Girard Guards. Its officers were Captain D.W. Hutchinson, First Lieutenant J. Godfrey, and Second Lieutenants Charles A. Pettibone and James E. Pettibone.

Locally, the men of Girard Township also served in the 4th U.S. Light Artillery Corp, Battalion A; the Pennsylvania 15th Calvary Division; the Pennsylvania 16th Calvary Division; or one of five infantry units: the 83rd Company C, the 111th Company H, the 145th Company H, the 250th Company C, or the 250th Company H.

The war was truly a brother against brother tragedy for the Kibler family of Girard. There were ten children in the Kibler family, nine sons and one daughter. Three sons fought with the Union forces during the war while two fought with the Confederacy. Henry Kibler served in the Union Navy and was Girard's first casualty. His brother Frederick, a salesman in the Deep South before the hostilities began, had many business contacts and friends there and ultimately served with the Confederacy. After the war, Frederick returned to Girard to live.

Another two such individuals were George and Richard Maynard, sons of Edward Cross Maynard, who lived at Springfield Crossroads (Routes 215 and 20) in Girard Township. The older of the two, Richard, a farmer by trade, enlisted into the Pennsylvania 111th Volunteer Infantry on February 12, 1864. During the first couple of days after he enlisted, Richard sent several letters home to his father from Camp Copeland, a training facility located near Harrisburg. The first written on February 14 from the camp reads:

> Dear father, as we expect to leave here to morrow I thought I
> would send you a few lines. I shall send my money in this letter

by Mr. Sweete. I have taken a receipt for it. The 109 regiment has arrived. There is a great crowd here. Rather too large for this place. I am getting along finely. I bunk with Charlie Walbridge. Tom Gibson came from Waterford and fetched along some butter apple butter and such and with the help of some other we made some very good meals. I send $65 to you. Given Mr. Swete I receipt fore it.

In haste
RL Maynard

The second is written on February 18, 1864 from the same place and reads:

To the Committee for the raising of volunteers for Girard township:
Pay to EC Maynard such bounty as I am entitled to receive from the township of Girard for enlisting on the quota of said town.

RL Maynard

The third letter written that week, again from Camp Copeland, was penned on February 20, 1864:

Dear Father,

I received your letter half an hour ago. I am glad you will be able to get the money. I sent you a letter a few days ago in which I enclosed a sort of receipt an order for you to draw my money. Also a receipt for my $65 dollars which I sent by Mr. Savert. Let me know when you receive it. You need not laugh at my order for twas my first produce. When you get my town bounty and my 65 dollars you know what to do with them and I want you to do it. We are having splendid weather here again I have got well. I had the mumps, my right ear swelled so I could not hear with it at all. The boys took care of me first rate. The first night I had the hardest fever I ever had in my life. Now I don't know how you feel about my being in the army. Wither you feel glad to get rid of me or wither you could stand it to have a nuisance at home again but I feel first rate, enjoy myself first rate. It is not a very good place to be sick in. I have had some photographs taken. I shall send one to John. They are not very good. I would like to know all the news from home, what you are doing, etc. I would like to have the rest of them write to me. They need not wait for me to write first. Write all the news you can. Send the paper if you are a mind to. I would like the Cincinnati times as well as any other paper I know of. Charley likes it here first rate. He goes to the 145th to Harry Harvey's company. Lewis Moon is here, yet the same old penny. A company of invalids come here a few days ago. The 105 was here but it has gone again. When you write tell me what you know about the 111th regiment. I don't know as I have anything more to write now so I remain with respect.

RL Maynard

Tell William and George not to enlist while there is a possibility of staying at home. One is enough to have in the army. Write soon. Write immediately."

Richard L. Maynard survived the war, although wounded in the leg, returned to Girard on July 27, 1865 after his enlistment was completed, and took up farming once again. In 1867, at the age of 22, he married Harriet Gudney. The couple had one child who died at birth. They remained in Springfield until their deaths, Harriet in 1913 at the age of 64, Richard in 1922 at the age of 77. Both are buried in the family plot in the Springfield Cemetery.

GIRARD

George Maynard, Richard's brother, did not heed his brother's advice discouraging him from enlisting. Sometime in March of 1864, George Maynard enlisted in Company K of the 145th Pennsylvania Volunteer Infantry and reported for duty. Like his brother, George wrote home to his family in Girard Township to tell them of the news while he was away. His first letter arrived home in April, written on April 16 from Alexandria, Virginia. He writes:

> Dear parents,
>
> I had my picture taken and thought I would send it home and let you know where I was. I have seen General Lees house and Uncle ABE. There is not a fence any wares to be seen including of all the fortifications that we heard so much about. I enjoy first rate health so far and hope you enjoy the same. When I have time I will write a long letter that is a foot long or more.
>
> We expect to move soon so I can tell ware to write.
>
> George Maynard
>
> I hope you will not think that I had a pipe in my cap it is the Badge of our Corpse.
>
> Direct Company K 145Regt P.V.
> Washington, D.C.
> Geo. Maynard
>
> I shall write again soon I need not count on you to write. It is getting dark so I must quit and cook supper. Captain Deveraux is a first rate fellow.

Several weeks later, a letter dated May 12, 1864 arrived at the home of Mr. Maynard in Girard Township. The letter is from Henry (Harry) Keith, a fellow soldier and friend of George's. His letter is brief and to the point, but lacks vital information for George's family:

Dear Sir;

Mr. Maynard, by the request of George, I under to write you a few lines and know that he is wounded, but not dangerous. A ball in the calf of the leg. He haves the best of care. I can't tell you where to direct a letter but say he will write often. He is in spirits and if he get worse he will send for you. There has been a battle for eight days before he was wounded on the eighth day. I don't know where George lies.

HC Keith

Luckily, the family received a letter dated May 15, 1864 from Fredericksburg, Virginia a few days later. This one was written by George and goes into much more detail of his injury and his recovery, along with the fate of some of his friends.

Dear parents;

I write again although it is with fear that the news this counter will be a harder struck on you that is has been on me. I told Harry to say I received a flesh wound. Well it was flesh and bone. The ball struck me just above the ankle taken bone and all, so you see, off comes my leg. Now I have two legs minus part of one but don't fret it might have been worse. At least I have done all the fighting I shall. With exception of the wound I am well. I have concluded that a trade will do me after I get home. We shall start for Washington in a few days. There was a battle going for 6 days before I was wounded. I believe Captain Deveraux is dead. Cord is reported dead. They say our regiment could not muster 100 men. I have not heard from Fran George Allen since I was wounded. A battle is near. Bullets fly. When I get to the hospital I will write again. There's no use for you to write till you get another from me. Excuse my writing for as you must know I have said all I have but I will come out all right in the end. I believe Harry is all right or he was day before yesterday. So much for this lesson but I am thankful it is no worse because it don't deprive of me of a living or money.

Yours
George

Primary documents contained in the collections of the Erie County Historical Society relating to the Maynard family state that both Mr. and Mrs. Maynard were devastated by the news of their son's injury. Given their son's lack of education and previous occupation of farming, they were genuinely concerned about his future. Unfortunately, their concerns were short lived as is indicated by the next letter they received.

May 22, 1864
Fredericksburg 2nd Corp Hospital

Blessed Mother;
    Your bright boy fell asleep in Jesus an hour ago. His right leg was amputated and there were two bullet holes and two buckshot in the thigh alone while a ball had passed through his left hip. It was impossible to save him but he bore his suffering bravely trusting God and could not speak of his mother without choking.
    God granted me the privilege of doing what I could to fill your place from Sabbath evening. His mind wandered at the last and he left no message and this little book is all we found in his pocket.

Jane G. Swisshelm

The Civil War Era: 1860–1868

Jane G. Swisshelm was an active abolitionist and writer and editor of a small newspaper in the Pittsburgh area prior to the war. The paper achieved national attention as a result of its viewpoints and Swisshelm achieved national notoriety. Swisshelm personally knew Secretary of War William Stanton and pleaded him to allow her to join the women under Dorothea Dix who gave aid and comfort to the wounded soldiers. Secretary Stanton eventually conceded and appointed Swisshelm to the Fredericksburg Hospital, where she eventually encountered George Maynard. A month later, Swisshelm wrote another letter to Mr. and Mrs. Maynard describing their son's hospital stay.

June 20th 1864
Dear Mrs. Maynard;

I certainly thought that George died at peace with God or I would not have written as I did. I reached Fredericksburg on Sabbath evening May the 15th and was sent by the surgeons to the 10th division, 2nd corps. Hearing that this also was in the worst condition of any hospital in town I went there and there I found your son with our 80 other badly wounded men. Until Thursday I had no surgeon and no wardmaster and a set of mules who had to be watched night and day and the Drs. of Surgeon put me in charge of the building, so you can see that I could not do as much or learn as much of every man as I had like to do. But your son and three others attracted my attention as superior to most of the men. His right leg had been amputated just below the knee and he did not light of any other wound. I dressed the stump and found the amputation had been well done and he was so cheerful and hopeful I expected him certainly to get well. I got a little pillow for his stump and one for his head from the Christian Commission and two of the young men washed him and put a clean white shirt on him and a pair of barred flannel trousers, blue and red, and he looked so superior to the others that we laughed at him and called him an aristocrat and he talked about going back to the front when he got his wooden leg. I gave him particular care because he was one of the few I thought could be saved. I knew from his appearance, he had been tenderly brought up and must be muched loved by his parents but I always talk to the wounded man of hope in God and try to learn if they trust him and pray for the recovery or preparation for whatever may be his will. They all called me mother and he certainly told me when I thought he would get well and when he was very cheerful that he trusted God and thanked him for sparing his life and would serve him if he lived. That is I asked him question to that effect and he asserted. One day after being out I came and found him reading the 14th chapter of John's Gospel aloud to those who lay near him.

The day after while I was dressing his stump, he spoke of his other wound and I wished upon seeing it, cutting up the leg of the trousers I found, on the stump thigh on the back part, two bullet holes and two buckshot holes. I was angry with him for not telling me sooner of these wounds, but he was bashful and had not liked to trouble me as I was very busy. Next time I dressed these wounds he spoke of his "other wound" but said he did not like to have me see it. I thought it was in the groin and sent the only man I had who could dress wounds to dress it. Next morning I could see he was not so well. I told him I must know more about that other wound and when he told me it was his left hip. I had great difficulty in getting him moved so much on his right side that I could see it. Then I found that after he fell on the field a bullet had passed directly downward toward the knee leaving a hole clear through six or eight inches long. Then I began to feel that his chance of life was small for he must be flat on some of these holes. I got broad low benches about 4 inches high made for him and six others to get them off the floor, fixed his bed all I could to keep him off the wounds; but you will see how hard it would be even at home with every convenience. There I had to buy a frying pan from a woman and show the nurses how to put two boards across it to make a bed pan. He never complained, never appeared to suffer, only grow weak. Thursday we got him and eight others carried into the Catholic Church next door where it was higher and the air better. We got a surgeon but he always preferred to have me dress his wounds and would not let anyone else touch them if he could help it. Whenever I came in sight he called or tried to call me and it always appeared a great comfort to have me near him. I gave him wine and water ten minutes before he breathed his last. Once I asked him what word I should send his mother if he should not get well. He choked up and said "Oh don't! She could not bear it!" He never appeared to give up that he could die and leave his mother. He said very little, but this is what I thought he felt and for the last three days it was hard to understand his speech, as he gradually lost the use of his arms and his voice and hearing.

Wednesday the 18th
4 days before he died.

When I was leaving him in the night to go to sleep I was kneeling at his side fixing his pillow and tucking in his blanket and then said to him "now go to sleep but first say your prayers." He smiled and nodded assent. I said are you sure you say them and he said he was sure. "Then" said I "say the little one tonight that your mother taught you and I will say it with you" and together we repeated the Child's prayer "Now I lay me down to sleep." He clasped his hands reverently on his heart and closed his eyes as he said it. His voice trembled and the tears forced through the lids, but he did not speak loud. When we were done I said "now you believe that God will keep your soul for Christ sake and will take it to himself when you die no matter where that is." He nodded and said, but his voice was so full of tears he could not speak plainly, "yes" and I knew he did. I could read all in his face the words he was to modest to speak but "The hearer of prayer" heard that prayer, that night in the old church by the dingy white pillar and when at last he went to sleep, God took his soul—the soul committed to his care. No one ever sincerely asked God to save his soul and was refused. He asked it, asked it sincerely, and what did anybody ever do more. The day he died I was with him and he was trying to get up, trying to find something. I asked him what that was, he said he wanted to go "up the canal." He talked and talked but this was all I could understand for his speech was thick. He wanted to go, to go up the canal with William after his hat. He is buried somewhere in Fredericksburg, I cannot tell where but it is in Gods earth and when the savior comes in his throne, to judge the quick and the dead, He will have no trouble in find him.

I was sick when I went to Fredericksburg and have been dangerously ill since I returned and not in any hospital now and fear I shall not be able to go among the wounded now this summer. Thought is painful to me. I would rather be among them then occupy a throne. No one can owe anything for anything I can do for them for it is Gods work and the thought of this and the thanks of the men—the knowledge that the lives of them have been brightened by my care and the death of them made more hopeful is a award so ever great that I am infinitely the differ to Him who has granted me the blessed privilege. That you and I may meet your son in that other land, may God in His mercy grant.

Your sympathizing friend
Jane G. Swisshelm

Life for those families that lived here in Girard during the Civil War was not unaffected by this terrible conflict. The residents strove to maintain some sense of normality during an abnormal time. Diary entries depict aspects of daily life, as if nothing had changed. Edward Cross Maynard writes of traveling to Erie, of building fences, of selling hay at $30 per ton, selling pigs for $2.50 each, and selling potatoes for 50¢ per bushel. He writes about going fishing, sowing oats and timothy seed, and moving cows and horses from one pasture to the next. Yet at the same time, certain entries speak of only the war. For example, on Saturday, March 1, 1865, he writes about a Girard War Meeting and on Tuesday, March 7 about the list of drafted men posted at the Girard Station. He writes about sending Richard money and postage stamps, of picking up Richard's pay from the army, or of the reaction of the citizens of Girard the day President Lincoln was shot.

As a direct result of the war, prices in the town rose dramatically and for many families, attempting to purchase food became increasingly difficult. According to the *Girard Union*, commodities prices per bushel for July 4, 1862 were: wheat, $1.10 to $1.15; corn, 45¢; oats, 38¢; rye, 50¢; barley, 50¢; potatoes, 50¢; green apples, $1; beans, $1.25, hams, 7¢ per pound; cheese, 6¢ per pound; and eggs, 8¢ per dozen. This was close to four times the going rate only one year earlier.

In July of 1862, Brigadier General Daniel Butterfield summoned Private Oliver Wilcox Norton, of Springfield Crossroads, Girard Township to his tent. Norton was the brigade bugler and a member of the Pennsylvania 83rd Infantry. He recalled that evening's experience years later in a letter in response to the August 1898 issue of *Century Magazine*. The magazine contained an article entitled "The Trumpet in Camp and Battle" by Gustav Kobbe. Gustav Kobbe, a music historian and critic, wrote about the origins of bugle calls during the Civil War but admitted that he was unable to trace the origins of "Light's Out" or "Taps." The inability to locate the origins of this call prompted a letter from Oliver Norton on August 8, 1898. Norton, who was in Chicago at the time, claimed he knew how the call came about and that he was the first to perform it. In his letter Norton wrote:

I was much interested in reading the article by Mr. Gustav Kobbe, on the Trumpet and Bugle Calls, in the August Century. Mr. Kobbe says that he has been unable to trace the origin of the call now used for Taps, or the Go to sleep, as it is generally called by the soldiers. As I am able to give the origin of this call, I think the following statement may be of interest to Mr. Kobbe and your readers. . . . During the early part of the Civil War I was bugler at the Headquarters of Butterfield's Brigade, Meroll's Division, Fitz-John Porter's Corp, and Army of the Potomac. Up to July, 1862, the Infantry call for Taps was that set down in Casey's Tactics, which was borrowed from the French. One day, soon after the seven days battles on the Peninsular, when the Army of the Potomac was lying in camp at Harrison's Landing, General Daniel Butterfield, then commanding our Brigade, sent for me, and showing me some notes on a staff written in pencil on the back of an envelope, asked me to sound them on my bugle. I did this several times, playing the music as written. He changed it somewhat, lengthening some notes and shortening others, but retaining the melody as he first gave it to me. After getting it to his satisfaction, he directed me to sound that call for Taps thereafter in place of the regulation call. The music was beautiful on that still summer night, and was heard far beyond the limits of our Brigade. The next day I was visited by several buglers from neighboring Brigades, asking for copies of the music which I gladly furnished. I think no general order was issued from army headquarters authorizing the substitution of this for the regulation call, but as each brigade commander exercised his own discretion in such minor matters, the call was gradually taken up through the Army of the Potomac. I have been told that it was carried to the Western Armies by the 11th and 12th Corps, when they went to Chattanooga in the fall of 1863, and rapidly made it's way through those armies. I did not presume to question General Butterfield at

the time, but from the manner in which the call was given to me,
I have no doubt he composed it in his tent at Harrison's Landing.

For many families in the Girard area, participating in the war meant supporting locally established home front movements. Two of the major efforts taking place at that time were the United States Christian Commission and the United States Sanitary Commission. The United States Christian Commission was responsible for the moral and religious well being of the soldier. They provided Bible tracts and religious writings of various kinds to the troops as well as writing materials so that the soldiers could write letters home. In order to provide these materials to the troops, the United States Christian Commission relied on donations and monetary gifts from a variety of sources.

The role of the United States Sanitary Commission was quite different and thus allowed for greater participation in as a whole. Its role was to provide for the physical well being of the soldiers. The Relief Committee of the Woman's Pennsylvania Branch of the United States Sanitary Commission provided food, clothing, and other goods such as coal, which was used for heating, to the needy families of soldiers here in the Erie area. The local chapter of the Ladies Aid Society collected and packed donated items for distribution to the soldiers. They were in constant need of clothing, such as cotton or flannel shirts and drawers, slippers and socks; sheets, pillow cases and bed-ticks; pads for fractured limbs and wounds; fans and netting to protect from flies; housewives (period sewing kits), handkerchiefs, and wash rags. Food items such as oatmeal, farina, cornstarch, dried rusk, jellies, jams, soda biscuits, crackers, butter, onions, apples, cranberries, pickles, oranges, and dried fruits were also collected. Beverages and stimulants, such as good black tea, chocolate, syrups and lemonade, wine, and brandy were also collected and were offered to the sick and suffering. Good reading materials consisting of lively and interesting books, monthlies, pictorials, works of art, science, and literature along with any other item that could possible give comfort to the troops in the fields or hospitals were collected and accepted.

According to the *Erie Gazette* of December 4, 1862:

> The Ladies Soldiers Aid Society . . . forwarded on the 22nd of November, one box of hospital stores for the sick and wounded Pennsylvania volunteers containing the following articles. 10 1/2 pounds of lint, 85 bandages, 168 compresses, 5 quilts, 2 pair socks, 10 abdominal bandages, 9 shirts, 9 sheets, 25 towels, 11 pair drawers, 12 handkerchiefs, 6 pair slippers, 1 linen coat, 7 bran bags, 1 bag dried currants, 30 pounds dried apples, 1 pair pillows and cases, 1 can currant juice.

The gathering of goods was considered vital by all the residents of Erie County and they took pride in their efforts. The July 31, 1862 edition of the *Erie Gazette* states:

> Erie County has contributed largely to the comfort and relief of our country's sick and wounded soldiers in the way of "Hospital Stores." Probably no county in the state has contributed more, in proportion to the population. From this point, supplies have gone chiefly to the General Aid Society at Cleveland—a society honestly and ably conducted and consequently worthy of the fullest confidence. The number of boxes sent from this city alone must be upward of thirty. The expense and trouble attendant upon getting stores to Washington has prevented our ladies from sending directly to that city. To get a single box there, by Express, costs from $7 to $10. We make this statement because it seems to be supposed in some quarters that we are not doing our share in the truly patriotic work referred to.

At some point in time, Asa Battles Jr. was called to service and hired a substitute to serve for him, which was a common practice at the time. His brother, Rush Battles, by all indications was never drafted and on March 28,

1861, married Charlotte McConnell Webster, the daughter of James Webster, a prominent mercantile operator in the community. Charlotte McConnell Webster's cousin, Charlotte Rebecca McConnell, would marry Dan Rice later that year. Both Rush and his new bride wrote in their diaries of the day's events. Rush writes: "Thurs 28 Weather dry, pleasant. Married at half past 10 and left on noon train for Hornelsville. Arrived there at 10:00 pm," while his new bride pens a few more sentiments: "28th Thursday. The day of my wedding. Rush and I now married about half past ten and left on noon train for Hornelsville. Mother beautiful. I trust it may indeed from indication of our married life I hope I feel a sense of its duties & responsibilities and trust I shall endeavor faithfully to discharge those duties."

The newly wedded couple traveled the Deep South, stopping in Atlanta, Savannah, Macon, Chattanooga, Memphis, Raleigh, and Charlottesville before returning to Girard in late April. On May 1, 1861, they began constructing a new home, north of Rush's grand Italianate home on the former Girard fairgrounds. Two years earlier, this was the site of the grand 1859 Girard Agricultural Fair, where over 120 exhibitors set up stands for the week's festivities.

The war had its effects on the local businesses of the Girard community. Folks living along the banks of the canal saw an increase in coal, iron ore, and other goods being transported along its lengths. Several businesses perished as a result of the southern states' succession from the Union and the formation of their own government. One in particular was Asa Battles Jr.'s mail contracting business with the post office. *The Cosmopolite* stated in an article dated September 5, 1889 that "he had contracts in the mid, western and southern states, on several of which he had established stage lines for passengers . . . owing to the unsettling of values, the war destroyed this business."

Sometime after the call for 500,000 men in July of 1864, Asa Battles Jr. was commissioned by Pennsylvania's governor, Andrew Curtin, to fill the state's quota by hiring "colored recruits" for the southwestern states. In this way Curtin had hoped to avoid another draft from the men within the commonwealth's borders. However, this attempt to fill the quota was unsuccessful and a second draft was issued. On the last two pages of Edward Cross Maynard's 1864 diary appears a list of every man from the area who was drafted into the army that year and indicates those who did not survive.

DRAFTED MEN		DIED
G Lloyd	Luvis Smith	RH Sanfred
J E Ryan	E Morris	H Simpson
H Daggot	CD Bennett	Jet Martin
John C Martin	JC Thompson	JW Phillips
H Kirkland	Wilson Wheaton	GH Hartson
Calvert Clark	RD Watts	Sam Rice
LM Barnes	H Babbett	P Sherman
Hemmingway	Alvin Anderson	S Godfry
WG Phillips	JS Sherman	N Phillips
WM Trout	Walter Strong	Geo Vansice
Jas Miles Jr	Jas Sampson	E Huidelar
J Hasler	Sam Barker	PM Sisson
Sam McClellan	DD Barnes	A Hartsteard
Abbe Hopkins	M Silverthorn	WN Anderson
R McClellan	John Whipple	W Seeley
Ed Barker	W C Culverson	CJ Young
JN Sherman	G Woolsey	L Laverage
H Stearns	Gus Davenport	HR Tellar
R Anderson	Lyman Poadger	O Miller
SR Hannan	Gus Keith	J Miller
JB Robbertson	Oscar Seeley	
JB Tuckey	TJ Rouse	
John Dodge	Mark Godfry	
Frank Muller	R Creamer	
C W Pettibone	L M Keith	

By 1864, Dan Rice had taken up an interest in politics and challenged the popular Republican state senator, Morrow B. Lowry, for the office. Rice ran as a Democrat and was eventually defeated. Few newspapers took his candidacy seriously. The *Erie Weekly Observer*, the voice of the Erie Democratic Party, was an exception. On September 15, 1864, it published: "Rice would, if elected, enter the Senate with a practical experience of the world and a broad, comprehensive knowledge of the wants and duties of the people, possessed by few members of the body."

In January 1865, the third and final call for 300,000 men was issued. In order to fulfill this call it was necessary to hold a third draft. This took place in Ridgeway during which 2,010 names were drawn from Erie County. Of these, none were from either Girard Borough or Township.

Sometime in 1865, Dan Rice, the notable circus performer, arranged to have a monument erected within the borough limits to honor the Civil War dead of Girard. That monument, which still stands in the center of Main Street today, is said to be the first of its kind in the country. The base of this monument measures 8 feet square at the bottom, contains carved upright cannons in the corners, and supports a 17-foot-high Corinthian column draped in the American flag and topped by an eagle. The monument was designed by Leonard Volk, a famous Chicago sculptor.

A few of the locals objected when the borough council approved the site in June of 1865. They did not mind the national attention for the village or the fact that Dan Rice was paying the $6,000 in costs. The problem was the proposed site on Main Street, in front of Rice's mansion. They claimed that the monument would memorialize Rice's arrogance more than the honored dead. When they lost in council, the opposed residents sought a court injunction, which ordered council to reconsider. With the eyes of the country upon them, the members of council reconsidered, then re-approved the original site, and the work began on the monument. Not trusting that his adopted home would keep his civic memory alive, the showman had "Erected by Dan Rice" chiseled on the base of monument a week after unveiling.

GIRARD

On a picture perfect day, November 1, 1865, the monument was dedicated. *Harper's Weekly* reported the event to the country with a cover story. Special excursion trains brought as many as 10,000 people to the little village, "the largest and most enthusiastic assemblage of people ever held in this section of the country." Not one to waste a crowd, Rice ended his season by giving two shows in Girard that day. After the morning performance, a noon salute of 13 guns sounded throughout the village. Rice drew up his animals and wagons for a parade that began at 1:00 p.m. with the band chariot and its carved swans. This was followed by a carriage of veterans of the War of 1812 and then marching soldiers of the recent conflict. Masons, Odd Fellows, and the fire department joined in full regalia. The most admired float was an elephant-drawn wagon carrying the Daughters of Freedom, 36 young women representing each of the reunited states.

The dedication ceremony began with a local general praising Rice's loyalty. Governor Andrew G. Curtin of Pennsylvania gave the principal address; letters from President Johnson and Generals Grant, Meade, Sherman, and Hancock were read; and the former Ohio governor, David Todd, made a few remarks. The ceremony concluded with the laying of a wreath at the base on the monument by two of the Daughters of Freedom, the young ladies representing Pennsylvania and South Carolina.

Several biographers of Dan Rice claim that Rice personally knew Abraham Lincoln and had invited Lincoln to the event and that Lincoln had accepted. What an interesting turn of events could have transpired for the little town of Girard if Lincoln had not been assassinated earlier that year. Lincoln after all was very familiar with the quiet town of Girard. According to *Following Lincoln's Footsteps*, a book by Ralph Gary, Lincoln had stopped briefly in Girard on February 16, 1861 as he was zigzagging across the Midwest. Lincoln said a few words to the gathered crowd as he did at all stops in an attempt to calm the nation's rising fears. Sadly, Lincoln's body also passed through Girard during the early morning hours of April 27, 1865 on its way to Cleveland as his funeral procession wound its way home to Springfield, Illinois, the final resting place for the President.

Continued on page 105

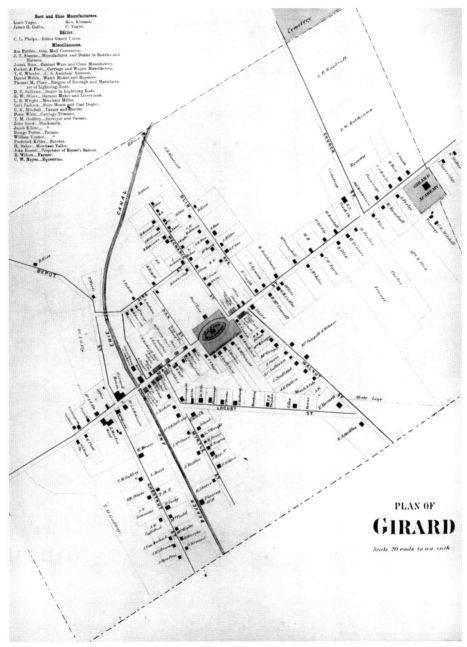

1865 Plan of Girard—The 1865 Atlas lists the various businesses and residences of the town of Girard.

Asa Battles Sr., born April 10, 1786, moved to the Girard area in 1824 with his wife, Elizabeth Brown Battles, and their four children. (Photo courtesy of the Erie County Historical Society.)

Rush Battles hired a local carpenter named Erastus Slater to construct this Italianate home for himself and his family in April of 1858. The final cost was $550 and an acre of land. (Photo courtesy of the Erie County Historical Society.)

The R.S. Battles Bank was constructed in 1893 by Rush Battles from locally produced steel, stone, and brick. The bank had a colorful history, including remaining open for business during the Great Depression. (Photo courtesy of the Erie County Historical Society.)

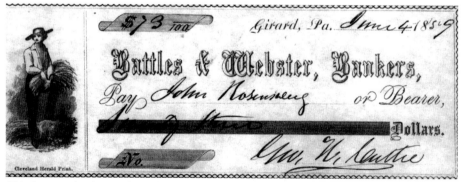

This is a rare bank note from the Battles & Webster House of Banking that was established by Rush Battles and Henry Webster in 1859 in the town of Girard. The bank continued operations until 1946 when it voluntarily merged with the National Bank of Girard to form the Battles Girard National Bank.

Another view of the Rush Battles home. (Photo courtesy of the Erie County Historical Society.)

This view shows East Main Street in 1895. (Photo courtesy of West County Historical Association's Hazel Kibler Memorial Museum and Community House.)

This picture of the Pennzoil Gas Station was taken in 1950. (Photo courtesy of West County Historical Association's Hazel Kibler Memorial Museum and Community House.)

November of 1956 brought one of the fiercest snowstorms to ever hit the borough. Here is Main Street at the end of the storm. (Photo courtesy of West County Historical Association's Hazel Kibler Memorial Museum and Community House.)

This view shows Main Street in 1890. (Photo courtesy of West County Historical Association's Hazel Kibler Memorial Museum and Community House.)

This view shows West Main Street in 1890. (Photo courtesy of West County Historical Association's Hazel Kibler Memorial Museum and Community House.)

This view shows Girard's downtown Main Street region, taken in 1990. (Photo courtesy of West County Historical Association's Hazel Kibler Memorial Museum and Community House.)

Charlotte McConnell Webster Battles was instrumental in providing a new school for the Girard community in 1910 by donating $35,411 towards its construction. (Photo courtesy of the Erie County Historical Society.)

The school guards at Battles Memorial School pose for a picture in 1950. (Photo courtesy of West County Historical Association's Hazel Kibler Memorial Museum and Community House.)

The first railroad station in the township was erected by the Bessemer Railroad in North Girard. (Photo courtesy of West County Historical Association's Hazel Kibler Memorial Museum and Community House.)

Construction of a new trestle over Elk Creek for the Bessemer Railroad occurred in 1858. The crossing was 15 feet high and 1,400 feet long and remains in use today. (Photo courtesy of West County Historical Association's Hazel Kibler Memorial Museum and Community House.)

This view of the town's Civil War Monument, street trolley, and the Methodist Church was taken in 1920. A tornado that struck the area in 1952 destroyed the church's bell tower. (Photo courtesy of West County Historical Association's Hazel Kibler Memorial Museum and Community House.)

Charles Barber, a prominent lawyer in Washington, D.C., married Charlotte Elizabeth Battles on October 21, 1875. Unfortunately, for reasons unknown, the couple divorced a year later. (Photo courtesy of the Erie County Historical Society.)

Charlotte Elizabeth Battles was born to Rush and Charlotte McConnell Webster on October 11, 1864. This photo was taken in 1885 just prior to her marriage to Charles Barber. (Photo courtesy of the Erie County Historical Society.)

Charlotte McConnell Webster married Rush S. Battles on March 28, 1861 in a quiet ceremony in Girard, Pennsylvania. The couple raised their family within the borough and became the most prominent family in Northwestern Pennsylvania. (Photo courtesy of the Erie County Historical Society.)

Culbertson Mill, located on the east bank of Elk Creek in West Girard, was first built in 1814 by Peter Wolverton. W.C. Culbertson ran the mill during the late 1800s. (Photo courtesy of West County Historical Association's Hazel Kibler Memorial Museum and Community House.)

The dam across Elk Creek provided the necessary water power to run the various mills and trades located along its banks. (Photo courtesy of West County Historical Association's Hazel Kibler Memorial Museum and Community House.)

This locomotive was produced by the Climax Locomotive Company in Corry, Pennsylvania. Because of its gearing, being built for power rather than speed, the locomotive changed the logging and mining industries. (Photo courtesy of the Erie County Historical Society.)

This view shows Dan Rice's carriage house. (Photo courtesy of West County Historical Association's Hazel Kibler Memorial Museum and Community House.)

Dan Rice's house stood in the center of town. The house was moved to the corner of Vine and Wall Streets to become part of the American Legion. The statues still exist on the borough building's lot. (Photo courtesy of West County Historical Association's Hazel Kibler Memorial Museum and Community House.)

This portrait of young Dan Rice was taken around 1860 prior to his marriage to Charlotte Rebecca McConnell. (Photo courtesy of Randy Marshall.)

The Erie Extension Canal brought Dan Rice to Girard in 1854. In June of 1868 he appeared in his famous red, white, and blue outfit at the Democratic Convention held in New York City. He had aspired to become the national Democratic candidate but lost the nomination to Horatio Seymour, who eventually lost the presidential election to the Republican candidate, Ulysses S. Grant. (Photo courtesy of Randy Marshall.)

The Dan Rice House, North Girard. The Dan Rice House was located across from the railroad depot in North Girard from 1871 to 1876. (Photo courtesy of West County Historical Association's Hazel Kibler Memorial Museum and Community House.)

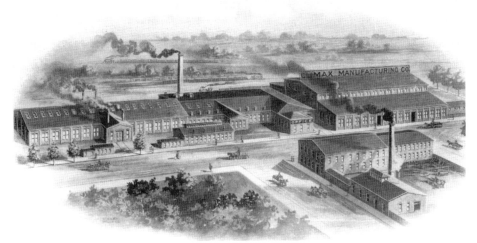

The Climax Locomotive Company in Corry, Pennsylvania was owned by Rush S. Battles. (Photo courtesy of the Erie County Historical Society.)

Denman Theatre is located on Main Street in Girard. (Photo courtesy of West County Historical Association's Hazel Kibler Memorial Museum and Community House.)

Elizabeth Brown Battles was the wife of Asa Battles Sr. The couple moved to the Girard area in 1824 from Chautauqua County, New York. (Photo courtesy of the Erie County Historical Society.)

This view shows the surrounding Elk Creek Valley. (Photo courtesy of West County Historical Association's Hazel Kibler Memorial Museum and Community House.)

This horse-drawn fire pumper was the first mechanical fire apparatus purchased by the A.F. Dobler Hose Company on March 12, 1900. (Photo courtesy of West County Historical Association's Hazel Kibler Memorial Museum and Community House.)

The first mail delivery employees of the township pose with the postmaster as Rural Freight Delivery was established for the residents. (Photo courtesy of West County Historical Association's Hazel Kibler Memorial Museum and Community House.)

This 1914 view shows the Foster House, named for Stephen B. Foster. (Photo courtesy of West County Historical Association's Hazel Kibler Memorial Museum and Community House.)

This view shows the Girard Day Parade in 1911. (Photo courtesy of West County Historical Association's Hazel Kibler Memorial Museum and Community House.)

The first passenger train to pass through the borough limits was a Knights Templar excursion train on the Pennsylvania, Shenango, and Lake Erie line on June 15, 1891. (Photo courtesy of West County Historical Association's Hazel Kibler Memorial Museum and Community House.)

The Girard Wrench Manufacturing Company was organized in 1875 and employed 75 workers to manufacture adjustable wrenches, many of which still exist today. (Photo courtesy of the Erie County Historical Society.)

In the early 1900s, the Battles Vineyards provided employment for many of the town's residents. In this photo, workers pose outside of the Myrtle Street Grape House. (Photo courtesy of the Erie County Historical Society.)

This is a view of the Girard Hotel located on Main Street and Rice Avenue prior to the devastating fires in the 1940s, which resulted in the removal of the third floor. (Photo courtesy of West County Historical Association's Hazel Kibler Memorial Museum and Community House.)

Workers are pictured at Girard Manufacturing Company. (Photo courtesy of West County Historical Association's Hazel Kibler Memorial Museum and Community House.)

Workers are pictured at Girard Manufacturing Company. (Photo courtesy of West County Historical Association's Hazel Kibler Memorial Museum and Community House.)

Workers are pictured at Girard Manufacturing Company. (Photo courtesy of West County Historical Association's Hazel Kibler Memorial Museum and Community House.)

November of 1956 brought one of the fiercest snowstorms to ever hit the borough. Here is Main Street at the end of the storm. (Photo courtesy of West County Historical Association's Hazel Kibler Memorial Museum and Community House.)

Henry Webster joined forces with Rush S. Battles in 1859 to establish the first bank in Girard, the Battles and Webster House of Banking. This business later evolved into the R.S. Battles Bank. (Photo courtesy of the Erie County Historical Society.)

Henry Hall's News Stand was located on East Main Street. (Photo courtesy of West County Historical Association's Hazel Kibler Memorial Museum and Community House.)

A.J. Hayes Garage opened on West Main Street and Vine Street. (Photo courtesy of West County Historical Association's Hazel Kibler Memorial Museum and Community House.)

Gudgeonville Bridge spans Elk Creek. (Photo courtesy of West County Historical Association's Hazel Kibler Memorial Museum and Community House.)

This view shows Miles Bridge, North Girard. (Photo courtesy of West County Historical Association's Hazel Kibler Memorial Museum and Community House.)

Finnish workers lay new train tracks across Main Street for the new Pennsylvania, Shenango, and Lake Erie Railroad in 1888. (Photo courtesy of West County Historical Association's Hazel Kibler Memorial Museum and Community House.)

Reverend Charles Shipman was the boss conductor of the Underground Railroad in the Girard area and pastor of the Universalist Unitarian Congregation. (Photo courtesy of West County Historical Association's Hazel Kibler Memorial Museum and Community House.)

Rush Sobieski Battles was the youngest child of Asa Battles Sr. and Elizabeth Brown. Born April 24, 1833, he became the most prominent figure in Northwest Pennsylvania. (Photo courtesy of the Erie County Historical Society.)

The town and township were named after Stephen B. Girard, pictured here, a Philadelphia philanthropist who owned land in the surrounding area. (Photo courtesy of the Erie County Historical Society.)

George Dougherty ran this advertisement on May 23, 1836 in the Erie Gazette. *Dougherty was the first businessman to set up shop in the new borough.*

This house on South Creek Road is where Denman Thompson was raised. (Photo courtesy of West County Historical Association's Hazel Kibler Memorial Museum and Community House.)

This view of Luce & Thompson Mercantile was taken in 1880. (Photo courtesy of West County Historical Association's Hazel Kibler Memorial Museum and Community House.)

The 1960s brought a new telephone network to the Girard community. (Photo courtesy of West County Historical Association's Hazel Kibler Memorial Museum and Community House.)

The Webster family gathers at their grandfather's home on Main Street for a portrait in the early 1900s. (Photo courtesy of West County Historical Association's Hazel Kibler Memorial Museum and Community House.)

This view shows the Atlantic Gas Station taken in 1950. (Photo courtesy of West County Historical Association's Hazel Kibler Memorial Museum and Community House.)

The railroad trestle built in 1852 over Elk Creek collapsed under its own weight. It was rebuilt in 1858. (Photo courtesy of West County Historical Association's Hazel Kibler Memorial Museum and Community House.)

This picture of H.A. Traut's store was taken in 1880. (Photo courtesy of West County Historical Association's Hazel Kibler Memorial Museum and Community House.)

Members of A.F. Dobler Hose Company participate in the 1911 Girard Day Parade. (Photo courtesy of West County Historical Association's Hazel Kibler Memorial Museum and Community House.)

This view shows West Girard from the top of the hill. (Photo courtesy of West County Historical Association's Hazel Kibler Memorial Museum and Community House.)

The Sacred Heart Mission House was located on the east edge of the borough. (Photo courtesy of West County Historical Association's Hazel Kibler Memorial Museum and Community House.)

This picture of Well's Park in downtown Girard was taken in the 1950s. (Photo courtesy of West County Historical Association's Hazel Kibler Memorial Museum and Community House.)

The weight of the snow from the storm in November of 1956 was so great that it collapsed the roof of the local skating rink located on Myrtle Street. (Photo courtesy of West County Historical Association's Hazel Kibler Memorial Museum and Community House.)

This photo was taken in 1900 and shows the mouth of Elk Creek, which continues to be a popular recreation area today. (Photo courtesy of West County Historical Association's Hazel Kibler Memorial Museum and Community House.)

Continued from page 56

Girard can lay claim to several national celebrities of the time. Charles Stow, a nationally known editor and poet, located to the borough in 1867 and spent each winter there with his family until his death. Frank Drew Sr., the famous comedian, also claimed Girard as his home. Another name nearly forgotten today, but huge in show business in the mid- to late 1800s, was Denman Thompson, who was born in the township. His stage presence and his character parts on the stage were legendary. The play he wrote, entitled *The Old Homestead*, has probably only been surpassed in performances by recent productions of *My Fair Lady* or *Cats*.

Originally born in 1833 in Girard, "Denny" Thompson ran away from his New Hampshire home at the age of 17 to join a circus, where he performed a song-and-dance routine. At the close of the circus season he made his initial stage appearance in a Boston theater. In 1854 he played small parts for several weeks in a stock company at Cleveland, Ohio. Next he went to Toronto, Canada, where he became a member of the Royal Lyceum stock company from 1855 to 1868. He played Irish, Negro, and Yankee characters in a large number of productions, eventually landing the role of Uncle Tom in Harriet Beecher Stowe's anti-slavery production *Uncle Tom's Cabin*.

In the early 1870s he appeared in a sketch written by himself called the "Female Bathers," which served to introduce a Yankee farmer on a visit to New York City. It was rather suggestive, and many first rate theatres refused to book it. About 1876, the sketch was rewritten and lengthened into a four act play. Thompson toured the country for 10 years in this play, meeting with unbounded success. The press and pulpit alike showered glowing reviews on the production. Dissatisfied with the somewhat flimsy nature of the play, Thompson engaged a newspaperman to write a new vehicle, which would retain some of the character and general theme of the old one. The result was *The Old Homestead*, which was given its premiere in Boston in 1886. During the 22 years that Thompson toured the country in *The Old Homestead*, the total box office receipts were more than $5 million.

In May of 1898, at the close of the regular theatrical season, Thompson presented *The Old Homestead* at the Kibler Opera House in Girard. The show was not "cut" but was performed in its entirety and then some. Both matinee and evening performance were given and the box office receipts totaled $700, of which Thompson received $420. Before leaving town he turned part of his profit over to the Wilcox Library fund. Doing so, he said, was the most pleasurable act of his life. Denman Thompson died in 1909 and was buried in Swanzey, New Hampshire at his ancestral home.

The second bank in the borough, the First National Bank, was organized in 1863, by Henry McConnell, James Webster, Henry M. Webster, R.S. Battles, John Gulliford, and L.S. Wright. Henry McConnell was elected president, a position he filled to the close of his life, in 1871. James Webster succeeded him to this position, which he filled until the charter expired in June 1882. R.S. Battles was elected cashier and occupied that position during the entire administration of the concern. A.W. Course was elected assistant cashier and held the post until November 1871. He was succeeded by C.F. Webster, who filled the position to its close. Henry M. Webster was elected vice president at the retirement of James Webster and occupied this post until his death. During the panic of 1873, all other banks suspended payment in currency, while the two banks located in Girard paid all their demands in currency on presentation. The First National Bank was in a prosperous condition and had passed successfully through all the periods of financial distress. The charter having expired prior to the passage of laws by Congress, it was closed 1882. It paid off its stockholders by giving them 20¢ on the dollar inside of 30 days.

The thoroughfare known as Rice Avenue was opened about the same time as the establishment of the North Girard Post Office in 1863, or perhaps a little later. Dan Rice established a company, on paper, to build a horse railway from Girard Borough to the village. *The Girard Spectator* reported on March 2, 1866:

> We have been shown a copy of an act passed by the legislature of
> this state empowering certain citizens of our village to form a
> company to build a horse railway from the village of Girard to the

new town of Dan Rice, formerly known as Girard depot. The site
of the proposed railway will commence at the Academy, running
along Main Street to the road intersecting that street leading to
the depot, following said road the whole distance.

Nothing ever came of the Girard and Dan Rice Horse Railway Company; omnibuses were operated throughout the borough instead.

On December 30, 1864, a serious fire broke out in the borough, destroying an entire block. George Kibler's, Jake Kibler's, and James Cross's buildings burned. The three buildings housed two barber shops, Becker's clothing store, a 5 and 10 cent store, a dental office, a doctor's office, a tin shop, a harness shop, a butcher shop, two barns, and several second floor dwellings that were instantly demolished. The town quickly banded together to lend money and support to erect new buildings in their places.

In 1867, Dan Rice consolidated his two newspapers, *The Girard Spectator*, formerly the *Girard Union*, and the *Conneautville Crisis* to create *The Cosmopolite*, explaining that the name meant "Citizen of the World." Rice had purchased the *Girard Union* several years earlier because of its very outspoken support against Rice's earlier political campaigns. The *Conneautville Crisis* had been founded at Conneautville by T.G. Fields, under the auspices of Dan Rice, to advocate his election to the Presidency. Charles Stow, Rice's adman, became editor of *The Cosmopolite* and infused such a degree of vigor and ability into it that it earned a reputation the country over.

Just a few days after the birth of his second child, Dan Rice Jr., in late June of 1868, Dan Rice attended the Democratic convention in New York City as a hopeful for the presidential nomination. He appeared in his famous stars and stripes costume, which had become a popular patriotic symbol for "Uncle Sam." Rice lost the nomination to Horatio Seymour, who lost the election to the Republican presidential candidate, Ulysses S. Grant.

Some of the borough's historic buildings constructed during this period that still stand include The What-Not-Shop located at 18 Main Street East.

GIRARD

This wooden structure was built in the 1860s as the original site of Josiah Nece's Cabinet Shop. Later, R. Emmett Hanson operated his Harness & Carriage Shop. William H. Edson's house located at 16 Walnut Street was constructed around 1861 as the personal residence of William H. Edson, a local carpenter and builder. The Chauncy Brown house, located at 170 Locust Street, was constructed around 1860 by Chauncy Brown, a local carpenter and farmer.

The Universalist Church built on 107 Myrtle was a replacement structure erected by the Universalist congregation in 1867. The congregation built this Greek revival structure after their original building burned. The congregation was an active participant in the Underground Railroad during the American Civil War.

The Kessel Block (202 Main Street West) and the Rockwell Block (146 Main Street West) were erected to replace their predecessors after a fire in 1864. J. Kessel was a barber and later joined H. Becker in the tailoring business and occupied the second floor. The lower half was C.F. Rockwell & Co.'s mercantile business. Rockwell began selling dry goods, groceries, and crockery in 1852 and was a prominent businessman for over 50 years. Simmons Saddlery, located at 136–140 Main Street West was the site where John T. Simmons operated a saddlery and harness making business from 1863 through the end of the nineteenth century. By 1876, he had expanded his business to include trunks, whips, blankets and more. The Union Block, 69–71 Main Street West, was constructed by John Gulliford Jr. in 1868 to carry on his father's hardware business, which was established in 1839. Located in the west portion of the building, Gulliford sold silver, hardware, and furniture. David M. Olin, Myron Hutchison's son-in-law, ran a business in the east portion that sold woolens.

Chapter Five

THE MANUFACTURING ERA
1868–1880

No book about the Girard area could be considered complete without some reference to the Gudgeonville Bridge. The bridge is the oldest covered bridge in the county and probably the most picturesque and best-known area covered bridge. The Gudgeonville Bridge crosses Elk Creek just south of Girard in western Erie County. It has possibly the strangest history of any bridge in the world. Legend has it that about 1855 there was a Kentuckian named Obadiah Will, who was delivering a mule named Gudgeon to somebody in Meadville. He stayed overnight in Girard at the old Martin House. When he left the next morning, he was told to follow the road just west of Elk Creek on through Cranesville, which would take him right to Meadville. A couple of miles south, he got off on another road which took him to Gudgeonville. (At that time, the settlement had no name.) It was only a short distance from the covered bridge that spans Elk Creek to the old Beaver and Erie Canal, which was abandoned in 1871.

Just as Will and the mule got on the bridge, a couple of canal boats came up from the south. They carried a circus, and one of the boats was a calliope. The man who operated the calliope began to play a tune—"My Old Kentucky Home." Perking up his ears at the weird sound, the animal dug its front hoofs into some planks of the bridge and dropped dead in its tracks. The story was that the mule had been off its feed for several days—lonesome for Kentucky, perhaps. Will was given permission to bury the mule on the west bank of the creek, and he marked the spot with a large stone. He hired a painter to go out from Girard and paint the word "Gudgeonville" on each end of the bridge. That's how it got the name.

GIRARD

When Dan Rice's circus returned to winter quarters at Girard, Dan was told about the mule and the calliope, and he wrote a sad tale of Gudgeon's demise. The bridge is said to have ghostly apparitions of a wagon and mule, and the sounds of a braying mule can often be heard at dusk.

However, the region is also home to yet another real-life chilling tale. The surrounding area of Gudgeonville is composed of a sheer cliff made up of slit shale and is locally known as "Devil's Backbone." At least two children have fallen to their deaths in that area and their untimely deaths have resulted in the reporting of screams in the middle of the night from the local inhabitants.

At the conclusion of the Civil War, many of Girard's families continued to prosper. The discovery of oil in southwestern Pennsylvania in August of 1859 continued to attract a wealth of investors to that region. In the spring of 1872, George W. Kibler and several others organized the Girard Oil Company. They sunk a well on the Barnes property near Oil City and struck oil, bringing in as much as 100 barrels a day. It is documented that Asa Battles Jr. also owned oil producing wells and a refinery in Oil Creek. His brother's business partner, Henry Webster, was a member of Oil City's Oil Exchange where he was admired. The *Oil City Derrick* reported about Webster on March 15, 1872, "From the time of his first connection with the oil business he had been quite successful." However the town's involvement in this industrious enterprise would not last long.

In 1870 the oil industry was gradually being taken over by John D. Rockefeller of Cleveland. Rockefeller was one of the earliest recorded investors in the oil industry and had built a refinery in Cleveland. Determinedly, he began to squeeze out his competition with the hopes of monopolizing every phase of the oil production business. In early 1870, Rockefeller had joined forces with several other businessmen from his home town to create the Standard Oil Company and named himself president. By the year 1872, all interests in the Oil Creek region that were owned by the residents of Girard has been purchased by the Standard Oil Company.

By 1870 the population of the Girard Township had reached 2,018 and the national census listed the population of the borough as 704. The Girard

Hotel was built on the corner of Main and Rice Avenue. The three story building had the capacity to house 64 people in its 32 guest rooms located on the second and third floors. The ground floor housed a four star restaurant and meeting hall.

The St. Johannes congregation of the Evangelical Lutheran Church was organized in 1866 and subsequently purchased the church building formerly occupied by the Methodist Episcopal Society on Locust Street across from the United Universalist Unitarian Church in 1868. The Methodist Episcopal Society erected its present building on Main Street at that time. The pulpit of the St. Johannes church was filled for periods by the pastors in Erie. By 1876, Reverend Gavehling served both this congregation and the one in Fairview Township.

In 1870, the small hamlet known as North Girard, locally known as Dan Rice, existed just north of the present limits for over two decades. This small village consisted of a store, a cobbler shop, a blacksmith shop, and a hotel. The hotel was known as the Depot House and was run by the McCully family. In 1871, A.M. ("Ad") Osborn took over the proprietorship of the hotel and was approached by Dan Rice, who offered Osborn $500 to rename the hotel the Dan Rice House. As part of the deal, Rice gave Osborn three wooden elephants, which were mounted on the structure roof, one at either end and one in the center. The elephants remained on the roof until 1876 when Frank Lommer purchased the property and changed the name to the Lommer House.

On the night of September 5, 1871, Girard businesses suffered a serious blow that threatened both manufacturing and commercialism as the town knew it. The viaduct that carried the Erie Extension Canal over Elk Creek collapsed and the canal operation was brought to a sudden end. Emma Beigart, who lived near the site, wrote in her diary that the "noise was so deafening that it sounded like the end of the world was near." The canal company and its right-of-way had been previously purchased by railroad interests who were allowing it to fall into disrepair. Its demise was only a matter of time, but the end of the canal brought about the deterioration of the many small communities along its towpath that had organized and incorporated as a result of the business generated by the canal.

The Cosmopolite, after a brief suspension due to overall commercial depression that swept the country, was purchased by Jacob Bender and his brother Charles Bender in the spring of 1872. In the spring of 1873, Charles Bender went out of the concern but returned in 1876, and in 1880 Charles purchased the interest of his brother, who at the time was living in Erie.

In 1872, Rush Battles constructed a large barn on his property. The main building measured 78 feet by 54 feet and had an addition of 50 feet by 80 feet for the purpose of housing circus horses. An article appearing in the January 30, 1873 edition of the *Erie Observer* described the newly built structure:

> WINTERING STOCK—Brains and Mechanism vs. Raw Material—How a Girard Farmer Solves the Problem of Cheap Fodder. The "wintering" of stock in this climate, although a question which enters largely into the economy of farming and often determined the profits of the brief Summer season, does not receive from our agriculturists generally that conservation which its importance deserves and the careless hand of the feeder too often empties the bin which the industrious hand of the reaper has filled, while the richness of the barn-yard is actually littered with waste for which production cannot compensate. How then to keep stock from eating not only their own heads off, but those of their owners as well, is a problem second in importance to none set by Nature upon the broad acres for which reason we think we can do our farmer friends no better service than to record, as briefly as possible, the manner of its solution by one of their own number—R.S. Battles Esq., of Girard—and the advantage to be derived from a combination of brains and mechanism with fodder.
>
> In and adjoining the Borough of Girard, Mr. Battles has a farm, which a short time since was eaten bare in carrying but twenty head

of cattle through the Winter. Last year it supported 54 horses, 15 head of cattle and 150 sheep, with over thirty tons of hay to its credit in the Spring, and this Winter will have enough, and to spare, with the drove of horses increase to 130; that being the number of "pure Arabian steed" belonging to the showman, Mr. John O'Brien, whose Jack the Giant Killer stomachs Mr. Battles has contracted to distend during the Winter is such a manner that their frameworks shall be filled with something more substantial than light and shade, and prepared to again encounter the toils of the road the coming Spring. These are the toughest kind of subjects with which to wrestle on the feed question; and constitute a crucial test of Mr. Battles's system; which is based upon that prerequisite, a good barn; the main portion of which is seventy-eight by fifty-four feet, with an addition fifty by eighty feet. The immense stables on the ground are snugly ensconced between stone walls and ample feeding boxes, etc. Here the horses munch their fragrant messes safe sheltered from the tidal waves of cold. The main floor above their "tossing manes" besides being devoted to a granary and storage room, with spacious root cellar attached, contains the very life center of Mr. Battles's horse catering economy in the shape of a fine ten horse power engine, built by the Bay State Iron Works, of this city, the boiler of which, with a powerful steam pump, is honorably banished beyond the possibility of harm, to a brick boiler-room about five rods from the barn, where it asks no odds of insurance companies in warming itself with the rotten and refuse wood from the farm. On the floor above the engine, and connected there with belting, are a corn sheller, a straw cutter, a mill for grinding feed and the necessary gearing for running a first-class threshing machine. Here the daily rations of the quadrupedal borders undergo preliminary mastication by the tireless iron jaws which spout out the corn, oats, corn-stalks, straw and clover chaff, preparatory to their passage into a large upright cylinder, whence, after being wet down by means of the steam pump, they drop into a huge steam chest on the ground floor and are thoroughly cooked on high pressure principles. The result is a banquet fit for the centaurs, and at once the cheapest, and most nutritious and inviting ever set before an idle horse. Its component and proportional parts are 1 1/2 bushels cut feed, two-thirds of a quart of corn meal, and one-third of a quart of oat meal to each animal all that is fed—which allowance soon converts the travel-worn skeleton of the road into sleek, high-mettled chargers, who prance like colts when occasionally let out for a constitutional run. It will be understood that then cut feed is obtained exclusively from the materials regarded as even worse than useless is utilized to the greatest advantage. The recuperative merits of Mr. Battles's bill of fare have been treated with extraordinary severity by the horses now under his charge. Not only did they come in unusually fagged out, even for show stock, but while in this condition were attacked by the epizootic, and yet today they are in such trim as to extort from that veteran circus agent Mr. Chas. H. Castle, the compliment that they are the best looking show stock he ever saw in Winter quarters. The fears expressed that cut and steamed feed would make a horse soft and unfit him to take the road were effectually disproved by the result obtained with the show horses wintered by Mr. Battles last year, which held their flesh on the worst kinds of roads and long routes, from the start, developed unusual "staying" qualities all through an exceptionally hard season.

Mr. Battles also feeds his hogs steam-cooked food and obtains equally advantageous results therefrom. Recently the arrangements of his barn have been perfected by the introduction of an ample supply of pure water, which is forced to every part of the building by means of a ram.

Many old-fashioned, raw farmers will center their whole objection to Mr. Battles's system on the one plea that is costs too much. To this sufficient reply is that nothing is expensive which pays well, and it is sufficiently evident that Mr. Battles's investment has made him a larger return than he could have obtained in any other way from his farm. His system of feeding has stood the severest test to which it can be subjected, and, having completely triumphed, deserves the attention of his brother agriculturists in whose interest we have thus cursorily described it.

Farming was not restricted to large tracts of land within the township; rather, residents within the borough proper often raised small animals and kitchen gardens. Some residents prided themselves on their efforts and entered their accomplishments for judging in the various categories at harvest time fairs. In 1872, the Pennsylvania State Fair was held in Erie from Tuesday, September 17 through Friday, September 20. It was the first time that it had been held in Erie County and it created quite a stir. "Our own town seed deserted, having sent a very large delegation," commented the editor of *The Cosmopolite*. "It is estimated that on the last two days more people assembled on the grounds than on any former occasion in northwestern Pennsylvania. The receipts [were] larger than were taken even when the fair was held in Philadelphia. These are facts which speak well for the agricultural enterprise and liberality of the people of the northwest." There were many winners from West County that year; among them was Phillip Osborn of Girard Borough for his fall and winter apples.

That same year, news of a new invention offered by M.F. McIntire and James A. Webster reached the townsfolk of Girard. McIntire and Webster planned to manufacture their Atmospheric Washing Machines on a large scale and leased a local building for that purpose. They advertised that the machine would "operate with the greatest ease, use less soap, and make linens white." They further claimed, "Its cheapness and other meritorious qualities will soon secure its introduction into every household." The gentlemen sold the machine in two models, tin for $4 each and copper for $6 each, and were moderately successful in their enterprise.

The Panic of 1873 tested the strength of Girard's two financial institutions. The Panic began with the failure of the New York brokerage firm of Jay Cook & Company on September 18. By the end of the day, 37 other banks and brokerage houses had closed their doors. Two days later, the Stock Exchange closed and suspended all trading for ten days. This was the beginning of an economic condition that had been building since the end of the Civil War and eventually led to a depression lasting five years. *The History of Erie County* published in 1884 states that during the panic "all other banks suspended payment in currency, while the two banks located in Girard paid all its demands in currency on presentation."

The lingering effects of the depression that followed the Panic of 1873 were felt by everyone in the borough, including Dan Rice and his circuses. His poor management of money coupled with decreasing attendance created serious financial conditions for the showman. He had already lost *The Cosmopolite* and was forced to sell off or forfeit all his other parcels of property. One was an acre lot on the corner of Olin Street that was sold to James Webster Jr. to be held "in trust for a company being organized for the manufacture of wrenches at Girard." Webster bought a second acre adjacent from Truman and Bell M. Godfrey, plus a portion of "the canal bed, banks, towing path, and slopes and all appertenances at that point" from William L. Scott of Erie. The land had been amassed on behalf of the Walton Brothers of Cleveland, Ohio. The Walton Brothers, with a capital of $8,000, combined with the financial backing of the people of Girard, who owned one-half of the stock, and erected a plant to manufacture six styles of adjustable wrenches in 1874. The plant began producing wrenches utilizing the G.B. Phillips patent of August 1, 1871. The enterprise was first named the T.B. Walton Company and then later renamed the Walton Wrench Manufacturing Company. The wrenches they produced were of remarkable quality and obviously expensive to manufacture. This high cost was the main reason the company failed in 1875 and was sold at sheriff's sale.

The fledgling company was purchased by William C. Culbertson, who was named president, C.F. Rockwell, Charles F. Webster, and Rush S. Battles, who was named secretary-treasurer. This new company, under a limited partnership, was very successful and soon the Girard Wrench Manufacturing plant employed about 75 men. The new group surmised that a less expensive, less refined article would stand a better chance in the marketplace. The company began manufacturing a model following the design and appearance of the original Coes wood-handled monkey wrench, which at the time was past its patent validity. These "Girard Standard" wrenches were produced during the company's heyday and numerous examples still exist today.

In 1874, Asa Battles Jr., an entrepreneur who had tried his hand at numerous occupations, tossed his hat into the political ring. His bid for a seat in the state assembly as the Independent Party candidate was unsuccessful. By March of 1877 Asa Battles Jr. became involved with the Girard Wrench Factory, acting as a traveling sales agent. He reported that the "orders on hand now cannot be filled in a month and still they come" and that it was his opinion that "the Girard company makes and sells more wrenches than any other wrench factory in the country."

In 1876, Henry Webster, one of the partners in the Battles & Webster House of Banking, received an appointment as a U.S. customs officer and was assigned to Buffalo, New York. Consequently, he retired and left all his banking interests to his partner, Rush Battles. By this time, Rush had been married to Henry's sister for 15 years. Rush, now being the sole owner of The Battles & Webster House of Banking, changed the name of the institution to the R.S. Battles Bank. In 1878, Rush Battles was appointed the president of the First National Bank of Girard, making him the president of both banks in the town. In 1882, the charter of the First National Bank of Girard expired and for some reason it was not renewed. Since Rush Battles was still president of this bank at this time, when it closed, the R.S. Battles Bank took over all its interests, accounts, and loans.

An article appearing in the *Erie Sunday Gazette* dated May 7, 1876 reveals the story of how North Girard was Erie County's only "Gretna Green": "This, being the first station out of Ohio, is a good place for Justice Theodore C. Wheeler. When two young Buckeyes wish to be made one, contrary to the science of arithmetic and the laws of their own state, all they need do is take the Atlantic Express, due here at 9:50 a.m., have the knot tied and slide back to Ohio on the Toledo Express, due at 10:50 a.m." The law requiring a license to wed was not enacted in Pennsylvania until 1885. Ten years earlier, Ohio passed the marriage license law, and couples wishing to avoid the delay and publicity, not to mention the expense, came over the line to have the deed performed. Since North Girard was the first scheduled town in which the Lake Shore trains stopped, the town quickly became a Gretna Green almost as famous as the town in Scotland where that kind of marriage originated.

The grove behind the Battles Farm was used by the citizens of town for recreational purposes. Large community gatherings would spontaneously erupt at the good will of the family. *The Cosmopolite* stated:

> January 1, 1876, the citizens of Girard in large numbers gathered there in a grand picnic. Music was furnished by the Citizens Cornet Band, who were uniformed in linen dusters and straw hats. Addresses were made by resident ministers and an original poem was read by Charles Stow. Dinner was served, as everybody came with baskets well filled. The day being an unusual one, some wore their summer clothing and straw hats. The thermometer indicated 70 degrees in the shade. January 1, 1877, was not celebrated in that way, for a violent snow storm had raged for three of four days and the snow was between two and three feet deep on the level.

In 1877 George Kibler, who had previously been involved in the oil industry, opened one of the most successful mercantile businesses in Girard. His store, which was located on Main Street, operated for 60 years. According to Walter Jack of the *Erie Daily Times*, the store became well known throughout the states of Pennsylvania, Ohio, and New York "because of its large variety of stock."

John Kibler, George's brother, was a telegrapher at the North Girard Station and had invented a product known as Daisy Fly Killer. This product was advertised to have many uses, but its most widely known use was as an embalming fluid when diluted with water. Unfortunately, due to the large iron deposits in local water supplies throughout the county, Daisy Fly Killer caused the skin, particularly the face, to glow. The eerie effect created at funerals soon earned the product an unfortunate reputation and the product was unsuccessful.

Later that same year, a "nickel plated" railroad organized under the name New York, Chicago and St. Louis Railroad Company laid east-west tracks across Girard Township, just skirting the borough's northern edge.

Christmas came early in 1877 for the residents of Girard when the *Pacific Express*, or "old No. 5" as it was known locally, of the Lake Shore and Michigan Southern Railroad pulled into Girard that winter day. The screeching of the locomotive's whistle could be heard over a mile away. As the train neared the station, the watching crowd could see billows of smoke pouring out of one of the cars. As the engineer, Johnny Lace, brought the train to a stop at the water tank, the car was quickly uncoupled from the train. The engine leaped forward, pulling the blazing car to an adjacent siding where it was quickly uncoupled from the engine. Upon getting clear the engine backed up onto the main line, coupled on to the train and proceeded on its way.

The messengers in charge of the car worked heroically to save as much of the car's contents as possible. Sacks of paper-covered novels, published by the Seaside Library Company, were tossed out of the car into the snow at a hurried pace. These packages were eagerly seized by the spectators before the messengers could intervene. Thus was the beginning of the first circulating library in the town.

By 1880 the population of Girard Township had grown to 2,338 while the U.S. Census gave Girard Borough a population of 703. Jacob Bender, enumerator of the 1880 census, gave the following results for the area:

> With the exception of one person, a mulatto, the population is all
> white. In sex it is singularly evenly divided, there being 1,168

males against 1,170 females. The acreage in tilled land is 13,845; permanent meadows, pasture, orchards, etc., 2,920; woodland and forest, 3,582; total, 20,347 acres. The principal crops are wheat, oats, barley, corn, buckwheat and potatoes. Total value of farm productions of all kinds, $217,080, divided among 240 farms.

The appraisement of 1880 gave the following results: Value of real estate, $1,354,587; of personal property, $47,523; money at interest, $51,355.

The mills and factories of the township—not naming for the present those of Girard Borough, Lockport and Miles Grove—are as follows: On Elk Creek—Strickland & Nason's grist mill, at the mouth of Spring Run—the West Girard Grist, Saw, Cider and Plaster Mills, and a planning mill at the same place. On Spring Run, T. Thornton's woolen mill and Brown Brothers; hand rake factory and cider mill. A grist mill is said to have been established on this stream by Mr. Silverthorn, as early as 1799, being one of the first in the county. On the West Branch—Pettis' saw mill; on Brandy Run, Rossiter's tannery; on one of the lake streams, Herrick's and Godfrey's saw mills. All of the above are run by water, but in some cases steam is also employed in the dry season. Pettibone & Morehouse have a limekiln on the lake road north of Girard.

The schools are fifteen in number, and as follows: Fairplain, on Lake road east; Clark's, on Lake road, farther west; Miles' near railroad junction; Cudney, on Ridge road west; Robertson, on Ridge road west; West Girard, in that village; Girard Station, at Miles Grove; Osborne, on Ridge road east; McClelland, two miles southeast of Girard Borough; Porter Bridge, one mile south of West Girard; Anderson, on Lexington road; Fair Haven, on same road further south; Blair, on Creek road three miles south of Girard Borough; Miller, on Old State road near Lockport; South Hill. Besides these there is a Union School on the Franklin Line, occupied jointly by that and Girard Township. The schools within the borough limits consist of a series of graded schools, managed by a Principal and three assistants. The schools opened in the fall of 1879, with an enrollment of 160 pupils under the superintendence of J.M. Morrison, who had three lady assistants. There are four departments, each of which is in excellent condition.

The hotels of Girard Borough are the Avenue House, finished in 1879, and owned and kept by Peter H. Nellis, and the Martin House, which has been in operation thirty years, and is now kept by Alonzo White. Girard has been rather unfortunate in the matter of hotel buildings, the old Girard House, which occupied the site of the present Avenue House, and the Central House of Joshua Evans, which stood on the east side of the public square, having both been burned.

In the fall of 1880, a well was sunk near the planning mill for the purpose of securing gas for lighting purposes. After boring 1,310 feet, and receiving an insufficient supply, the derrick was removed to a different locality and the second well is under operation at this writing. Besides this establishment, H.H. Waitman has a planning mill, and there is a small furniture factory. All of these concerns are run by steam. There is also a small bedspring manufactory owned by H.P. Malick located nearby.

The late nineteenth century brought industry to the lives of the Girard residents. This new industry would forever change their way of existing. The beginning of the industrial revolution would bring new jobs and careers to the small town, promoting the decline of the agrarian lifestyle that they had grown accustomed to.

Chapter Six

THE DAWN OF THE NEW CENTURY

1880-1904

By 1880 the population of Girard Township had grown to 2,421 while the U.S. Census Bureau gave Girard Borough a population of 703, nearly all of whom were engaged in some form of agricultural pursuits. One such pursuit was begun by Asa Battles Jr., who was buying tracts of land in Girard Township despite his other business interests. Most of these parcels were located between South Creek Road and Elk Creek. He named this large parcel of land "Pleasant View Farm" and it was on this land that his interest in fruit farming began. Eventually, his farm grew to be referred to as a plantation and he gained the reputation of "fruit culturist" in the region.

In the May 18, 1911 edition of *The Cosmopolite*, the following account of an earlier visit to Asa Battles Jr.'s farm was reprinted:

> We think Girard can claim the most extensive fruit orchard in the county, if not in northwestern Pennsylvania. Asa Battles, one of our own citizens, has on his farm, a short distance from town, 3,000 apple trees, most of them just coming into bearing; 1,500 pear trees, many of them being full of blossoms and giving promise of a fine crop of fruit. We also observed he had 1,000 peach trees, 500 quince trees as well as 3,000 grape vines.

The orchard and vineyard were on the same parcel along with "a fine tract of woodland," which protected the fruit crops from both the extreme west and north winds. Asa Jr. described how "great care has been taken to secure all the best varieties of fruits of each kind and the entire use of the land is devoted to the orchard." He permitted no other crops and kept the soil "well plowed and cultivated to keep it clean and mellow which can cause the trees to make an extraordinary growth each year."

Another reported visit in late October mentions that both the grapes and apples were being harvested. Asa Jr. grew mainly Concord, Catawba, Isabella, Iona, and Hartford Prolific grapes, proclaiming all other grape varieties "inferior and not worth the effort." He often sold his fruit to merchants in Meadville, sending them by wagon three times a week and reporting sales of $40 to $60 per trip.

In late May of 1880, the bones of a mastodon were turned over with the spring plowing on the Palmer farm on South Creek Road in the township. It was estimated that the creature was 15 feet long and 13 feet high, excluding the tusks. A reporter for the *Erie Observer* visited Girard and reported that the bones were distributed all over town. He described the vertebrae "of this mammoth mammiferous pachydermatous animal" being so large that it made Dan Rice's old elephant Hannibal look like a baby. Two zoology professors had arrived to investigate the find. The town became wrapped up in the publicity and the proprietors of both the Avenue House and the Martin Houses were asking their visitors if they wanted their "mastodons unhitched." Waiters asked diners if they preferred their mastodons broiled, roasted, or fried and even beer was sold by the "mastodon." The *Erie Observer* added that "The Mastodon Mutual Insurance Company Unlimited is about being organized and a new piece of music called The Mastodon will soon be ready for the band." Within three months, the discovery was all but forgotten.

Rush Battles by this time had many lucrative business ventures both inside and outside the township limits, one of them in Corry, Pennsylvania. In the late 1860s, the firm of Gibbs & Sterrett Manufacturing Company was making mechanical mowers and reapers. By 1872, it was obvious that the company had insufficient funds to continue operations and had no choice but turn to the city for help. In the spring election of 1873, the citizens approved the issuing of ten year municipal manufacturing bonds totaling

$106,000 and bearing eight percent interest. But with the panic later that year, the business still did not realize a profit. Attempting to gain renewed business, the firm changed its name to the Climax Manufacturing Company and began to manufacture engines and other machinery, but the company continued to falter.

On April 1, 1883, the city's manufacturing bonds came due and the city had no money to pay them. A suit was brought against the city by the largest bond holder, and Judge Galbraith of Erie decided that the issue was contrary to law and ruled against the bond holders. However, the matter was taken up with higher courts and the decision was reversed on the grounds that the bond holders were innocent parties and therefore entitled to recover their losses. The city accepted the decision and worked out a compromise with the major bond holder, which eventually led to the sale of the Climax Manufacturing Company. Others were paid off in the same manner with all loans being repaid in 1911.

Having recently acquired the failing industry at a sheriff's sale, Rush ceased all operations at the Corry plant, retrained the workers, and began the production of the geared locomotive. The geared locomotive was efficient in lumber operations, coal mines, fire-clay banks, stone quarries, and numerous other industries because of its design. The locomotives could easily handle a grade of 13 percent per mile as a result of their gearing ratio. Between 1888 and 1928, Climax produced 1,000 locomotives, which were a valuable key to the lumber industry's growth by making new areas accessible to large scale timbering.

According to the *1884 History of Erie County, Pennsylvania* by John Elmer Reed, "The whole [Girard] township is a splendid fruit country and many acres have been planted to grapes and strawberries." He further notes that the strawberry crop is just as important in Girard as the grape crop is in North East, Pennsylvania and credits Asa Jr. with growing 14 acres of strawberries that year.

Not to be outdone, his brother Rush planted the inherited family farm predominately in potatoes, corn, wheat, and barley. There were about two dozen fruit trees making up his small orchard in which he grew apples, pears, peaches, cherries, and plums, along with a small vineyard consisting mainly of Catawba and Isabella grapes with Concords being introduced in the late 1880s. Lucina Battles, Asa Jr. and Rush's sister, kept a diary in which she often mentions picking grapes and the fruits and using them to make jams and jellies as part of her housekeeping chores.

However, not all of Rush's farm interests lay in crop production. He cultivated horse chestnut trees, black walnut trees, and some rare ornamental trees and shrubs on the property. One of these, a Paulonia, native to China, was planted just south of the elaborate farmhouse near the granary. It grew to be over 40 feet high before it was stuck by lightning in 1952. The tree still remains on the property today and has heart shaped leaves and fragrant violet blossoms in the spring.

In the *1884 History of Erie County, Pennsylvania*, John Elmer Reed listed the following section:

> PUBLIC MEN. Girard Borough and Township have furnished a goodly proportion of the public men of the county. Among the number have been George H. Cutler, State Senator from 1873 to 1875, Speaker of the Senate, then the second highest office in the Commonwealth, from the close of the session in 1874, and President pro tem. during the session of 1875; Theodore Byman, member of Assembly in 1848; Leffert Hart in 1849; Henry Teller in 1860 and 1861; George P. Rea in 1868 and 1869; H.A. Traut, from 1883 to 1885; Myron Hutchinson, Associate Judge, from 1841 to 1850; James Miles, from 1851 to 1856; S.E. Woodruff, District Attorney, from 1853 to 1856, and United States Register in Bankruptcy for the Congressional District from 1867 to 1879; James C. Marshall, Prothonotary, from January 13, 1839, to November 16, 1839, and Samuel Perley, from 1851 to 1854; Jeremiah Davis, County Treasurer, from December 1, 1856, to December 23, 1858; L.T. Fisk, County Superintendent of Public Schools, from 1866 to 1869; Myron Hutchinson, County

Commissioner from 1828 to 1830, and James Miles, from 1835 to 1838; D.W. Hutchinson, Mercantile Appraiser, in 1877; William Biggers, Jury Commissioner, from January 1, 1880, to January 1, 1883; George Platt, County Surveyor, from 1872 to date; John Hay, Director of the Poor, from 1853 to 1857; James Miles, County Auditor, from 1840 to 1843, and Philip Osborn, from 1864 to 1867. Senator and Secretary of the Interior Teller, of Colorado, was a resident of Girard Township while a boy. The Girard members of the bar are James C. Marshall, D.W. Hutchinson, S.E. & T.S. Woodruff, Rush S. Battles, George H. Cutler and C.J. Hinds. Mr. Marshall moved to Erie in April, 1844, and the Messrs. Woodruff about 1872. Capt. Hutchinson was Chairman of the Democratic County Committee for several years, was a Delegate to the Democratic National Convention of 1872, and has represented the county frequently in State Conventions. In addition to the above officers, T.C. Wheeler was United State Assistant Assessor, being appointed under President Lincoln, and holding the office nine years. Mr. Osborn was keeper of the Marine Hospital at Erie, a State appointment, for several years, ending in 1883.

In 1886, a most controversial event rocked the little town of Girard: the marriage of Charlotte (Libbie) Elizabeth Battles, daughter of Rush Battles, to Charles E. Barber, a junior counsel lawyer from Washington, D.C. associated with Benjamin F. Butler. Butler was a controversial general in the American Civil War who was later elected by the people of Massachusetts to serve in the senate. In 1884 he was nominated by several Republican groups to run for President. However his campaign ended abruptly when he was accused of conspiring with Charles A. Dana, the editor of the *New York Sun*, to pull votes away from the Democratic candidate, Grover Cleveland.

Without advance notice, Charlotte Elizabeth married Charles at her parents' home on Walnut Street and then boarded the early evening eastbound train towards Washington, their new home. *The Cosmopolite* announcement described Barber as a lawyer of high repute with a lucrative practice.

In May of the following year, a small item in the local news column informed the townsfolk that "Mrs. Charles E. Barber of Washington arrived here Saturday. She will spend the summer with her parents." Almost immediately rumors began to indicate that something had gone wrong with the marriage. Charlotte Elizabeth's second cousin, Rebecca McConnell Rice, who was living in Rockford, Illinois at the time, wrote that she too had heard the rumors:

> Our most earnest hope is that Libbie may be fully vindicated and that man receive the punishment he so richly deserves. . . . it is a most beastly attack. . . . He has overreached himself and gone so far beyond reasonable limits that his case is a perfect farce. . . . his charges are distorted villainous stories. . . . Even now I cannot comprehend why he allowed his true character to become known at so early a period in his married life. . . . If money was his object in marrying Libbie I am sure he would have faired better by treating her well. After he had got her, in his power what his motive could be in getting up a thing of this kind is something I cannot understand at all. I am very thankful that he had a man like Rush to deal with instead of one he could take advantage of.

What exactly happened between Charlotte Elizabeth and Charles is not known and may not ever be truly discovered. However, what is known is that the members of the community of Girard accepted her back into their circle. Rebecca concluded in her letter "As far as I can learn the people of Girard have more charity in this matter than usual, with them, as the general feeling seem [*sic*] to be sympathy for Libbie and indignation against Barber for bringing such absurd charges against her, as well as total disbelief of the same."

GIRARD

In 1887, Asa Battles Jr. retired from many of his business ventures and, living quietly on his Pleasant View Farm, announced on July 7, 1887 that he was the official Erie County agent for the Benedict Berry Harvester, a new machine. He informed the local editor of the newspaper that "one person with the Harvester can gather as many berries as 10 pickers in the same time." All accounts seemed to indicate that this business, like so many before, was less than successful.

In May of 1888, the community of Girard was once again devastated by a massive fire that completely destroyed the Girard Wrench Factory, putting close to 100 employees out of work. The fire started in the roof rafters and the efforts of the fire company, which was inadequately equipped, were confined to saving the boiler and the stock room through the use of a bucket brigade. Losses to the owners were estimated to exceed $30,000 dollars beyond insurance coverage. The owners vowed to rebuild, which they did, and the company resumed business a year later. They began work on the "Girard Standard" wrench with its round handle design, which was offered in seven sizes ranging from 6 to 21 inches. In 1890, they began producing a bicycle wrench to help diversify their existing line. Around 1900, the company introduced its "Railroad Rough" or "Girard Special," which offered a more durable cast steel handle.

By the late 1880s, Girard's manufacturing base had grown considerable. The records boast two grist mills (Strickland & Nason's and West Girard, both in Girard Township), one tannery (Rossiter's in Girard Township), six saw, shingle, lath, and heading mills (West Girard, Gudgeonville, Pettis's, Herrick's, Shipman's, and Godfrey's, all located in Girard Township), one cider mill (West Girard Cider and Plaster in Girard Township), two planing mills, sash, door, and blind factories (West Girard in Girard Township, and one at Girard Borough), one woolen, carding, and fulling mill (Thornton's in Girard Township), one brick and tile works (West Girard in Girard Township), two wooden articles factories (Brown's Hand Rake Factory in Girard Township and Girard Furniture in Girard Borough), and four miscellaneous plants (Girard Wrench Factory, Miles Grove Iron Foundry,

Denio's Agricultural Tool Works in Miles Grove, and Pettibone's Limekiln in Girard Township).

However, George W. Kibler was not satisfied at the rate of the town's development. At his urging, a Board of Trade was organized to bring new business into the borough. Several of the more prominent businessmen of the community formed a committee "to show off the advantages of Girard in its true light" to any industry considering a move to the area. As a result, in 1891, both a shirt factory and the Theo J. Ely Manufacturing Company relocated to Girard.

But the biggest news was that the Pittsburgh, Shenango and Lake Erie Railroad agreed to extend its tracks through the borough and build a new depot within the town limits in November of 1890. Through negotiations lead primarily by Rush Battles and George Kibler, the "Peasley," as it was known, had been persuaded by $25,000 in funds raised by various townspeople. The citizens of Girard were to furnish the right of way from the old aqueduct over Elk Creek through the borough of Girard and the necessary depot grounds. Also, the right of way along the old canal bed to the Nickel Plate railroad at Wallace Junction needed to be secured. It would be the fourth railroad line to cut through the township but the first to lay track through the borough. At the initial meeting, the citizens, numbering 36 in persons, subscribed for the stock in amounts ranging from $5,000 down to $100. Congressman W.C. Culbertson was the largest subscriber, owning almost $20,000 in shares.

The following month, 42 Finnish workers moved into the town to begin work on the project and began laying tracks in the path of the old canal. Working ten hours a day with picks, shovels, and horse drawn drags, the workers received wages of $1.25 per day. The laborers quickly bridged the gap over Elk Creek then moved on to the other jobs. The passenger depot and freight house were located one block north of the Avenue House (present day Girard Hotel), a siding was built that would be able to hold seven cars, and Main Street, from Dan Rice's monument to the new tracks, would be regraded. The first Peasley passenger train was a Knights Templar excursion train that went through the town on June 15, 1891. According to *The Cosmopolite*, the train was accompanied by "the roar of cannons, toots and whistles, and cheer after cheer from the immense crowd. . . . It can be truly said that the first through train was heartily welcomed. The demonstration was a credit to the Girard Board of Trade."

In 1890, *The Clipper* teased Dan Rice about his periodic announcements of returning to the show ring. However, in 1891 these rumors came true and "Old Dan Rice" announced the creation of "Dan Rice's Big One-Ring Show!" The roster was undistinguished and small, boasting a mere 20 performers. The show opened in mid-May in Jersey City with plans to take it into New England, California, and Australia, but Rice caught a severe cold and collapsed in the ring. He later returned to the ring but a storm knocked over the tent, ending Rice's comeback. He would return to his home in Long Branch, never to set foot in Girard again, not even to attend the funeral of his second wife Rebecca in 1895. Rebecca had divorced Dan in 1881, charging him with "willful and malicious desertion." In an interview with the *North East Sun*, Rice recounted his relationship with Rebecca. She had been a mere child in the care of a nurse when he first laid eyes on her and he watched her grow into a pretty young woman. She had been impressed with him and as time passed, their friendship grew into love. He "straightened her up and taught her to turn out her toes and dance." And through his attentions, "she became a country belle . . . and the belle of a country village, you know, is more conspicuous even than those in the city and usually possessed with more beauty and intelligence that the rest of woman-kind."

But Rebecca's parents objected to the marriage. "They said it was because of the difference of our social standings and because of the difference in our ages." He interpreted social standings as meaning wealth and claimed he had far more than her father at the time. As to their age difference he said, "She preferred to be an old man's darling rather than a young man's slave."

After his bankruptcy in 1875, the statues on his estate were scattered, a handful eventually being placed around the borough hall. The monument that he had bought and fought so hard to erect was nearly ignored. The town that he had put on the map wanted nothing to do with him or his immediate family. On February 22, 1900, Dan Rice died at his home in Long Branch.

On October 16, 1893, 60-year-old Rush S. Battles began building a new bank building from locally produced brick, stone, and steel at the urging of his daughter, Charlotte Elizabeth Battles. The building was considered fireproof, burglar proof, and "state of the art." The new building was constructed on a site on Main Street across from his existing business and was adjoined by a new community library, also under construction.

Rush spared no expense in the erection of the two story building. The foundation walls and exterior walls were 24 inches thick. Both the floors were constructed by laying 10-inch steel I-beams 24 inches apart. These beams were let into the exterior walls and mortared in place. The voids between the beams were filled with corbelled bricks 10 inches thick. The walls of the vault, located in the rear right corner on the first floor, were 36 inches thick and the floor and ceiling constructed by laying 10-inch steel I-beams next to each other. Two heavy steel doors protected the two large safes inside the vault room; the outer door being equipped with an elaborate time lock and alarm that was directly tied to the electric light plant and Dobler Hose Fire Company. Despite all of the "high tech" security, the first floor atmosphere remained rather homey with two fireplaces and one teller window.

The turn of the new century brought many changes to the residents of Girard. The population increased to 2,534 residents and the 1900 census reported that for the first time in history, Girard's number one industry was no longer farming but manufacturing. The borough boasted of an industrial zone situated right off Main Street yet easily accessible to the railroads and their sidings. The Public Works Department was created and consisted of the Electric Light Plant and the Water Department. The borough, having recently purchased 1 acre of land from Rush Battles, erected a water tower on the top of the hill, which would provide all the residents of the borough with clean, safe, and reliable water.

The A.F. Dobler Hose Company was organized on March 1, 1900 and named after Dobler because of his generous donation of $200 for the first piece of mechanized fire equipment; a hand pulled hose cart. At the organizational meeting George Hess was elected chairman and foreman; George Cox, president; and Glenn McClelland, secretary and treasurer. Sixty men were named to the active list to serve in the department for a period of four years.

On March 12, 1900, plans were made to purchase another hose cart from the Ashtabula Hose Company, along with boots, rain coats, speaking trumpets, and badges. The company held many fundraising activities throughout the year to raise money. Some of these included subscription lists, dances, suppers, minstrel shows, and skating parties. The members met every other month to conduct business that year.

During this same time, another company, the Citizens Home Company (locally known as Hooks), existed. There is no historical information on this department, but on March 8, 1904, the two departments merged to form the A.F. Dobler Hose and Ladder Company. The department was incorporated by the state on February 2, 1907. On October 1, 1972, the company was given a citation by the House of Representatives, Commonwealth of Pennsylvania, for 75 years of continuous and outstanding service.

During this time, Rush Battles considered expanding the Climax Locomotive Company and contemplated placing the boiler shops on his vineyard property between Walnut Street and Myrtle Street. But the grape market and anticipated yield for the year of 1901 changed his mind and he decided that the plant would remain in Corry. Rush later sold his grapes at 20¢ per bushel with a yield of 110,000 bushels that year, while New York grapes were only selling at 10–14¢ per bushel.

On March 31, 1904, the front page of *The Cosmopolite* read:

> R.S. Battles is dead! These words were passed from lips to lips in
> subdued and solemn tones on Monday morning. The community

felt a personal loss in the unexpected removal of one of the most prominent and active business men of the town.

His death came very suddenly and very unexpectedly. Without a sigh or groan he passed instantly over the line on Sunday evening, March 27, 1904. His death was doubtless due to Angina Pectoris—neuralgia of the heart. He was in his seventy-first year and the youngest of his father's family. He is survived by his widow, Mrs. Charlotte Webster Battles and his daughter Miss Elizabeth; also by three sisters and one brother.

Our highly esteemed fellow townsman had reached the goal of earthly ambition. A profitable and progressive business, a fine home and a charming family, the respect and confidence of the community, had placed him in a position to enjoy the Indian summer of his life. He had attained high distinction in the industrial and commercial world, and he was conceded to be one of the most prominent business men in Northwestern Pennsylvania.

Expression, spontaneous, appreciative and heartily, has been given by his business associates to the esteem in which they held the man with whom they counseled and planned. A liberal education, generous opportunity for travel, and a competence as the harvest of a life of industry, had enriched his mind and given him a well-earned influence over others.

His presence was exceptionally prepossessing, his spirit affable, his manners relieving, his judgment mature and worthy of respect. His temperament was genial, and he was at his best when among friends, the cares of life laid aside, for rest and recreation. Nobody ever questioned his probity.

His habit of mind was conservative and he was averse to change from the long established order of things, in which he had found satisfaction and edification. Mr. Battles will be greatly missed among us, which ever way we turn. For over two score years, he has been an active force in this community. He was known in all classes. His face and figure were familiar to all as he walked from his home to the bank. As a token of respect for his character, all business places were closed during the funeral services which were largely attended and conducted by the Reverend J.W. Reese.

With the passing of Rush Battles, the citizens of Girard saw the end of a great financial era. While things would certainly progress in the future, the town would not be the same without his presence.

Chapter Seven

A TIME OF CHANGE

1904–1929

The first decade of the new century was devastating to the Battles family. Less than a year after the family lost its patriarchal member, Lucina Battles, Rush's sister, died on March 19, 1905 at the age of 81. Lucina was the fourth of Asa Battles Sr.'s six children and never married. Her daily life was comprised of keeping a country farm house and exchanging visits with family and friends. She daily recorded the weather and the happenings of her life in her diaries. Everything from favorite recipes to the wages being paid to strawberry pickers was dutifully recorded. Her main interest lay in reading and the creation of a Library Association. She began collecting books as early as 1859 and finally in 1891, the Library Association was organized with Mrs. C.F. Rockwell as president, Charlotte Webster Battles as secretary, and Charlotte Elizabeth Battles as treasurer. Lucina served as the head of the book purchasing committee. In June of that same year, Robertson Wilcox, a former resident of Girard, died and left $5,000 to be used to establish a free library in Girard. The library was constructed in 1893 next to the new bank with its main entry facing Main Street and the name, Wilcox Library, above the door.

Four years later, Alcina Battles died at age 89 on December 20, 1909. Alcina, the third child of Asa Battles Sr., lived with her sister Lucina her entire life. Like her sister, she too never married, but unlike her sister, she made her living as a school teacher outside of Conneaut, Ohio. Upon her death, the grand Italianate farmhouse built on the edge of town on Walnut Street would never be home to the Battles family again.

Under the direction of Charlotte Elizabeth Battles, the house was leased out to the various tenant farmers and their families who cared for and worked the Battles farmland between 1914 and 1957. Martin Bauer was the first and was hired as the farm manager for 31 years. Bauer had been working for some of the other farms in the area when he married Crescent Koehler in 1914 and the two of them moved into the first floor of the old Battles homestead.

Bauer kept the farm in working order, caring for the animals as well as the land. He grew hay, wheat, potatoes, and grapes and kept cattle and horses. The Niagara, Concord, and Delaware grapes had annual high yields. Bauer and Crescent had four children born in the house, an infant boy who died and three girls. The girls spent their childhood playing in the hallway on the second floor amidst the splendor that had been part of the Battles family. The family moved out in 1945 when Elmer Graves moved in, followed by Jack Blood in 1948, Merle Brown in 1952, and finally Fred Belson in 1954. When Fred Belson moved his family out of the house in 1957, the house was boarded up and began to deteriorate. Years later, the grove behind the farm house was no longer used for community picnics, but in the winter, when the water overflowed from the stand pipe and turned into ice, all the local children came to slide down the hill at "Bauer's farm."

On March 23, 1910, at a special meeting of the borough school board, Charlotte Webster Battles, Rush's widow, donated $20,000 towards the construction of a brick building to serve as a new school on Main Street. The town's school, Girard Academy, had become overcrowded, dilapidated, and deteriorated over the last decade, and something needed to be done. The offer was made on behalf of Mrs. Battles by her brother, Charles F. Webster, on the condition "if they will erect this year a new brick school building on the present school grounds."

The board members accepted the offer and on May 30, they selected an architect, H.P. Beebe of Buffalo, New York. Later in August they accepted a bid from George Kratt of Lorain, Ohio to erect the building at a cost of $43,800. According to an article from the *Girard Herald*, upon learning of Charlotte Webster Battles's gift, "the people of Girard felt that a wonderful thing had been done for the town and the request was made that Mrs. Battles permit the building to be called the Battles Memorial School."

As the plans were made, one improvement after another was included until the contract price far exceeded the estimates. Charlotte Webster Battles, a progressive, community minded, well educated woman, added $15,411 to her first gift on the stipulation that the school should be kept up to a first rate rating with a course of study approved by the state, that a 4-acre field adjoining the original school grounds be purchased as a school playground and that the grounds be kept in good condition. The minutes of the board meetings reflect the constant decision making involved with the building of the new school. The interior finish was to be first quality red oak throughout except in the two story auditorium where it would be first quality poplar. The bricks were subject to Mrs. Battles's approval and the front of the building was to be set back 128 feet from the sidewalk.

The first day of school in the grand new building was Monday, September 25, 1911, although the work was not completed. Charlotte Elizabeth Battles, serving as a member of the Board of Trustees for the Girard School Board, headed a campaign to raise donations to have the school rooms decorated. Generous donations were received by the Culbertson sisters and Mrs. C.F. Rockwell. However, despite all the contributions to the building fund, there remained an indebtedness of $10,000 for which the board issued bonds during that school year.

The first graduating class was composed of six members on June 13, 1912. They were Marion Jackson, class historian, Esther Shutt, class statistician, Eva Strodmeyer, Helen Beckman, Emma Drew, and Milton Peter, class orator. In August of that year, the school board instructed the Gorham Company to make a bronze plaque to honor Charlotte Webster Battles's generosity and placed it in the main hall. It was installed in time for the dedication of the building on Monday, October 2, 1912. A new school board took office that evening and consisted of Charles M. Hutchinson, president; E.L. Hanson, vice president; Charlotte Elizabeth Battles, secretary; Mrs. W.T. Ryman, treasurer; and Ida Hart.

The old Academy remained on the property for use by youth related associations. It was home to the athletic association, the band, and even the

Boy Scouts for a while. It was not until the spring of 1918 that due to increasing cost of repairs the building was closed. It was sold to Charles Hauck for $105 with the understanding that he was to remove it and all debris from the property by September 1.

Ida Hart resigned from the school board in November of 1913 due to health reasons. Mrs. Ryman served until 1920, and Charlotte Elizabeth Battles served until 1927. In 1926, she and the other members of the school board voted to enter into a written agreement with the Board of School Directors of the School District of Girard Township to provide for the establishment of a joint high school. The Battles Memorial School was bursting with students again and a bigger, newer building was the solution. The new joint borough and township school, the Rice Avenue Union School, was built on Rice Avenue and opened in 1928. At that time, the Battles Memorial School was designated an elementary school, offering classes through eighth grade to children of the borough.

By 1961, the auditorium of the Battles Memorial School, which was used for many fine civic functions, was converted to classroom space due to overcrowding. Student enrollment continued to increase with a steady determination, forcing the school board to act once again. In 1964, the new Elk Valley Elementary School was completed and the Battles Memorial School became a middle school. Growing enrollment forced the school district to construct a new high school in 1974, delegating the Rice Avenue Union School as its new middle school while the Battles Memorial School was turned into administrative offices. In the wake of the 1977 devastating tornado that struck Elk Valley Elementary, the Battles Memorial School was used once more by 300 fourth and fifth graders for the remainder of the school year. In 1981, rising costs and expenses forced the relocation of the administrative offices from the Battles Memorial School to the new Girard High School and the building was put up for sale.

By 1920 the population within the borough had risen to 2,681. The largest employer at that time was the Girard Model Works, Incorporated, which operated from 1919 to 1922. Founded by Frank E. Wood, the company operated under other names; as Girard Manufacturing Company from 1922 to 1935 and then as The Toy Works from 1935 to 1975. But whatever it was called, the toy company in Girard had a long affiliation with Louis Marx.

In the 1920s, Girard Model Works produced toys under the Marx label, along with its own line of steel autos, trucks, and trains. Louis Marx had made an arrangement with the Girard toy company to sell their products "as is," or specially made to sell under the Marx logo. Marx toys and Girard toys are, for all intents, indistinguishable (a few of the Girard toys bore the slogan "Making Childhood's Hour Happier"). The Louis Marx Company produced a wide variety of tin toys, dolls, playsets, and games. They were also a major producer of electric trains in both O and HO gauges. In fact, it is a good bet that Louis Marx sold more trains than Lionel back in the day.

When the Depression hit, Girard Model Works was in serious trouble. Among other things, they owed Louis Marx a massive commission check for being an agent for them. Marx had accumulated a lot of his pay in stock. The employees also owned stock, so Louis Marx bought them out. He offered them 50¢ on the dollar value for their stock. Since they realized that the stock was probably worth half its value, they agreed to sell. This brought the Girard Model Works squarely into the Marx toy empire and it kept all the employees working through the Depression at a time when most companies were folding or laying off.

Louis Marx immediately set to work implementing his program for success. First was development of a better motor. They ran the motor continuously for months. When it finally failed, engineers examined it to see what went wrong. They replaced the bearings with better ones, and so was born the most reliable toy train motor ever made. Marx's business philosophy was simple—build it to last and make it as cheap as you can, so you can keep the price down. Marx trains were cheaper than competing products from Lionel and American Flyer. However, they were slightly smaller, less ornate, and less detailed. But blessed with a simple, reliable motor, these tinplate wonders were sold through five-and-dime stores, general stores, and small department stores throughout the country. They were priced half or less than competing Lionel products. That meant that during the Depression, while other companies struggled or even folded, Marx sold trains.

On October 25, 1920 the *Girard Herald* proclaimed "Charlotte McConnell Webster Battles, dead at age 85." Her obituary stated that she had allied herself with "every progressive movement that looked toward the up building of the community and of character." She was a charter member of the Wilcox Library Association and also the Travelers Club, which was an outgrowth of the Chautauqua Literary and Scientific Circle of Girard. She served the Presbyterian Church as a choir member, with the woman's organization, and in her generosity. She was enthusiastic, gracious, community minded, and generous.

When Charlotte Battles first became ill, her daughter Charlotte Elizabeth hired Addie Hannah as a practical nurse to help care for her. Eventually, Addie moved out and Charlotte Elizabeth's friend, Georgianna ("Nan") Read moved in. Charlotte Elizabeth had met Georgianna, a manicurist at a beauty salon in Erie, several years earlier. Georgianna was bright, pretty, and had a good business sense about her. Eighteen years the younger, Georgianna and Charlotte Elizabeth became the best of friends.

A terrible loneliness overcame Charlotte Elizabeth after her mother's death. She had cousins in Girard, but there was no one to share her life with except her friend. Georgianna learned to drive and the two began to go everywhere together—to Cleveland to shop and to see an opera, to Chautauqua, to California to tour the western sights and relax. The two ladies loved to entertain, if not in their home on Walnut Street, then in Brennan's Tea Room on East Main Street. They belonged to the long standing Ladies' Friday Bridge Club, whose members were the social leaders in town.

Chapter Eight

A NEW DIRECTION

1929-1952

The stock market crash of 1929 proved that basic business in this country at that time was unsound. Everything was affected as the economy began its relentless decline eventually ending in the Great Depression. Bank after bank began to flounder as depositors made heavy withdrawals of their accumulated savings. By the beginning of 1933, the banking crisis had reached massive concern throughout the country just as leadership was about to change hands.

Since the newly elected Franklin Delano Roosevelt could not agree with the current President, Herbert Hoover, on how to exactly resolve the crisis, the governor of Michigan proclaimed an eight day banking holiday throughout his state to alleviate some of the strain on the banks. However, the overall situation grew worse each day. *The New York Times* called for a statement from the President; and six other states imposed limitations on banking; but Roosevelt continued his silence.

Thursday, March 2 and Friday, March 3, 1933 brought the heaviest runs on the banks in history. Millions of dollars were withdrawn in gold each day and hoarded by people all over the country. President Roosevelt reacted by contacting every governor and requesting that they place moratoriums on their banks. During the night all the governors agreed and by early the next day, Saturday, March 4, 1933, all state and federal banks were closed, the New York Stock Exchange was shut down, and the inauguration day commencements began under a somber atmosphere. President Roosevelt later said in his inauguration address: "This is a day of national consecration. The only thing we have to fear is fear itself."

Utilizing his authority, he proclaimed "a bank holiday for all banks and a cessation of all banking transactions" on Sunday, March 5 to be in effect until Friday, March 10.

Locally, the R.S. Battles Bank, which was solely owned by Charlotte Elizabeth Battles at this time, also had its difficulties. Depositors, panicked by what was occurring, were also withdrawing their funds at alarming rates. When the President's order was proclaimed on March 5, Charlotte Elizabeth Battles was vacationing in California, as she regularly did each March. Upon receiving the news from her uncle, Charles F. Webster, who was the head cashier and who had managed the bank for many years, Charlotte Elizabeth Battles sent a telegraph to her uncle with her instructions. "Business as usual!" was all the telegraph said. News of the telegraph's message quickly spread throughout the small town.

On Monday, March 6, just before the appointed opening hour, Richard G. Kibler left his job at the Model Works and went to the bank to see what would happen. Richard recalled that just outside of the building there were four farmers, whooping and hollering, waiting for the bank to open. At the appropriate moment, the door of the bank swung wide open and the depositors rushed in. They demanded that all the money they had in the bank be turned over to them at once. It was! Then, just before they were about to leave, Charles Webster asked them "Now what are you going to do with all that money?" Richard Kibler watched as all four of them turned around and redeposited all but $5.

According to the *Erie Daily Times*, there were 1,147 banks in operation in Pennsylvania in March of 1933. All but one, the R.S. Battles Bank, closed. Even the other bank in town, the Second National Bank of Girard, complied with the closing order. It reopened briefly for limited business after March 10 until plans to merge with the First National Bank of North Girard were developed. The two institutions merged in 1934 to form the Girard National Bank.

Under the title "Girard Bank Says 'Pooh' to State and U.S. Closings Edict," the *Erie Daily Times* carried the local story on March 9, 1933:

The R.S. Battles bank . . . is in a class by itself during these hectic days of money famine. The bank, it is believed, is the only one in the state and one of the few in the country which remained opened for business during the past week. Explained C.F. Webster, cashier, "Ours is a private bank and neither the state nor national governments have any authority over it. . . . There was no reason to close."

On March 11, the *New York Times* printed: "there has been no banking holiday as far as the Battles Bank in Girard is concerned. Business has been transacted as usual, officials explained. The institute is neither a state nor a federal bank. It is private, operated on the same basis as a private or independent store."

When officials in Washington learned that the R.S. Battles Bank had denied the presidential order to close, they issued additional orders for the bank to comply immediately. Receiving such new orders from the office of the president, Charlotte Elizabeth Battles is said to have compiled a note at her desk in the bank that simply stated: "Mr. President, since I do not presume to tell you how to run the country, don't you presume to tell me how to run my bank. We're minding our business, you mind yours. C. Elizabeth Battles." Throughout the crisis, the R.S. Battles Bank never closed its doors and none of its depositors and investors ever lost any money.

Along with the financial difficulties of the time, 1933 brought the shocking news of murder to the small town. According to Steve Hudson, local historian on the subject, on August 4, 1933, a local veterinarian discovered the bodies of 70-year-old Johanna Beigart and 74-year-old Albert Beigart on their isolated farm near Elk Creek. Johanna, having been severely beaten, was found dead in the kitchen while her brother Albert was found in the barn, stabbed numerous time with a pitchfork, still alive. Albert was taken to the nearby hospital, but never recovered to identify his attacker.

The police immediately launched an investigation with the primary motive of robbery suspected. The Beigarts were suspicious of banks and were reported to have kept a large sum of money in their home. The house had been ransacked and less than $30 was discovered when the police arrived. County Detective Leroy Search and Constable J.O. Badders headed the investigation. More than 100 people were rounded up, including the Beigarts' own nephew, and interviewed regarding their knowledge of the brother and sister. More rumors began to fly as the town was all in a buzz over the brutal slayings.

A few days later, the Beigarts' nephew shot the family hound dog for failing to protect the family. The dog was found shortly after the murders locked in one of the rooms and police suspected that the animal could have identified the killer. This suspicious action on the part of the nephew made him the prime suspect in the investigation.

In late September, the case broke as a 26-year-old illiterate farmhand was arrested and charged with the murders. Thomas Smith, being held by Wesleyville police on an unrelated charge, mentioned the name "Lynn Sloan," an acquaintance of his under surveillance in connection with the Beigart murders, during questioning. The *Erie Times News* dated September 30, 1933 revealed the story: "Fiendish Murderer Also Admits Plot To Kill Third Victim . . . Thomas E. Smith, 26, Tells of Gruesome Slaughter of Aged Beigarts in Farm Home on Aug. 4; Implicated Half-Breed Indian; Reveals Plan to Bash in Brains of Girard Farmer So Man's Wife Could Collect $8,000 Insurance, Wed His Accomplice."

According to the newspaper, Smith had met the couple six years earlier while working as a farm hand on George and Hattie Luther's farm. As it happened, Hattie had been carrying on an affair with another hired hand, Lynn Sloan, a self proclaimed "Half-breed" Indian from the Cornplanter Reservation in New York State. Hattie Luther, anxious to be free to marry her new lover, had offered Smith and Sloan a portion of the proceeds from George Luther's $8,000 insurance policy if the two men would murder her husband. Thomas Smith initially confessed that he and Sloan had killed the Beigarts for their money and had planned to kill George Luther. However, the following day, Smith recanted his testimony saying he knew nothing of the crime. Police took Smith back to the Beigart farm where he almost immediately described the exact positions of the bodies and revealed other details that could only be known by someone with direct knowledge of the crime. Smith again denied that he had an accomplice or a motive, stating that he believed the devil had possessed him and caused him to commit the slayings.

In November of 1933, a grand jury freed Lynn Sloan and Hattie Luther, citing insufficient evidence of conspiracy in the alleged plot to kill George Luther. Thomas Smith was declared insane and was permanently committed to the Fairview Hospital for the Criminally Insane near Philadelphia.

Shortly thereafter, the businesses within the town's limits began to reflect America's love of the automobile and travel as places like McQuillen Oldsmobile, Maxson Buick, Taft's Drive In, Western Auto, Donaldson Chevrolet, A.J. Hayes Garage, and Pennzoil Gas Station lined the streets in an attempt to lure customers to stop. Other businesses and manufacturing plants within the town, now long gone, included Hulls Cigar Store, Reeses Family Center, Girard Plumbing & Electric Company, Crosby Appliance, Joanart Shop, Seebauhere Bakery, Girard Recreation, Girard Tool and Die, Girard Coal and Supply Company, Pyramid Oil Company, C.G. Wood Company, Lake Erie Foundry, Morlite Equipment Company, Girard Manufacturing Company, Madison House, Avenue Food Market, and Julio's Appliances. The town of Girard had become a perfect blend of manufacturing and retail businesses, which served the growing community's needs.

In early 1946, in an attempt to better serve the citizens of Girard, the R.S. Battles Bank closed its doors and merged with the Girard National Bank to form the Girard Battles National Bank. The bank had faithfully served the town's needs for 87 years and Charlotte Elizabeth Battles retired from the business world of Girard, although she continued to help out the community when it was in need.

On December 17, 1952, the headline of *The Cosmopolite* read "Charlotte Elizabeth Battles Dies at Age 88." The *Erie Observer* echoed the sentiments with its headline: "Miss C. Elizabeth Battles, Distinguished Girard Citizen and Philanthropist, Dies." The paper stated that "death claimed the life of one of Girard's most prominent citizens in the quiet hours of early Wednesday morning. . . . "

At the time of her death Charlotte Elizabeth was very much active in the community. She was a member of the Presbyterian Church where she taught Sunday school, a member of the Elk Valley Garden Club and the Elk Valley Daughters of the American Revolution. She was the honorary president of the Wilcox Library Board, a member of the Travelers Club, and one of the founders of the Civic Improvement Association. She and Ella Skiff had been appointed, on May 8, 1914, the first women to serve on the board of trustees at Edinboro Normal School, where she continued until 1928.

Since she had no legal heirs except for distant cousins at the time, Charlotte Elizabeth Battles left her entire estate to her dearest friend and live-in companion, Georgianna Read, approximately $3 million for distribution. Charlotte Elizabeth's many charities and philanthropic activities continued after her death because of Georgianna Read; like helping young people go to colleges and technical schools and the gift of a savings bond to every graduating high school senior at her church. Some work left unfinished by Charlotte Elizabeth's death Georgianna was persistent in completing. It had been Charlotte Elizabeth's desire to turn her grandparent's home, built in 1832 and located on Main Street, into a facility for the aged as a memorial to them. Charlotte Elizabeth had purchased the house in 1947, but because of an error in listing the frontage, the sale was not completed. Georgianna saw the transaction through and in January of 1957, it became the Webster Home for the Aged managed by the Presbyterian Church.

Chapter Nine

TIME SLOWLY PASSES BY
1952–1990

After Charlotte Elizabeth Battles's death in 1952, Georgianna Read continued to live in the house at 306 Walnut Street in a manner that many found strange and unusual. It was as though she wanted everything to stop and remain unchanged. She remained active in the Presbyterian Church and carried on the life that Charlotte Elizabeth had created for her.

She was often lonely and sometimes would call a friend to go riding. They would drive nowhere in particular, just use the opportunity to catch up. When television became popular, Georgianna chose not to buy a set. An invitation to see a special show was a social outing and she feared that if she had her own set, the invitations would cease. Georgianna remained alone in the house at 306 Walnut Street for 30 years. "She had a good business head about her until the day she died," remembers Wesley Herbol, a friend and advisor. During the last few years of her life, she was institutionalized three times with broken bones or internal problems. Each time she was determined to return to the Walnut Street house and did so, the last time in 1981.

The construction of the new highway, Interstate 90, began in 1956 and with its completion, began the eventual decline of the economic life that the citizens of Girard were so used to. The super freeway allowed the traveler the opportunity to bypass the quaint community's shops and stores, and for the first time in its history, the population growth began to stagnate. Actually the census reports that the population only increased by 19 people between 1930 and 1960. With 2,700 people residing in the borough and the population not increasing, the town began to lull into complacency.

GIRARD

About the most exciting news to strike the town was the telephone number change, which occurred in the early 1960s. The town had new telephone lines installed that no longer required operator assistance to place calls to Erie, Conneaut, or Ashtabula. Informational campaign boards could be found throughout the town encouraging the residents to call Gridley6-2836 to learn how the new system operated.

In November of 1965, to celebrate the 100th anniversary of the dedication of the Dan Rice Civil War Monument, Hazel Kibler, the local town historian, organized a grand celebration. Just as in the original dedication, 36 young women, dressed in appropriate 1865 fashions, represented the 36 states of the reunited union. The original dedication speech was read and once again a wreath laying ceremony was held at the monument. There was even a Dan Rice look alike contest held. The following year, the event was moved to August in hopes of better weather and became known as Dan Rice Days.

In the late 1960s, several community-minded individuals approached Georgianna Read hoping to secure funding to create a local history museum. Since she was the controlling force behind the town's most prominent family, they hoped she would agree. Unexpectedly, they were turned down on her premise that any local museum would have to include information concerning Dan Rice, which due to his marriage to young Rebecca was at odds with the Battleses. Therefore, she felt she could not oblige. Fortunately for the town, another individual shared their dream.

Hazel Kibler, born in 1884, was educated at Girard Academy and lived her entire life in the town of Girard. Her relatives were some of the original town merchants on Main Street and important members of the community; W.C. Kibler, her father; George Kibler, her brother; and Henry Tellar, her maternal grandfather, to name a few. Incidentally, George Kibler had the first phone within the town's limits. He strung wire from his house on Chestnut Street to the store on Main Street to the Battles Memorial School. Born in a Victorian home at the foot of Chestnut Street, Hazel Kibler began teaching school at Girard Academy at age 16. She eventually taught at

Battles Memorial School where her love for history developed. She was a member of the Elk Valley Garden Club, the Travelers Club, and the Literary Society and had received the Award Book of Golden Deeds.

During her modest life, she collected images and newspapers concerning the development of the town and its residents. Upon her death in 1973, the residents were surprised to learn that her will left $40,000 to establish a local history museum within the borough limits and a community house where local organizations could meet free of charge. She specified in her will that the museum had to be up and running within a year or the funding would revert to some other organization. Her will also left money to have all the headstones in the Pioneer Cemetery at Main Street and South Creek Road remounted and a memorial erected.

In the fall of 1973, the West County Historical Association was incorporated under the auspices of promoting local history. The newly founded organization then began looking for a suitable site for the Hazel Kibler Memorial Museum and Community House. It purchased the 1950 Cape Cod home with the half basement and garage on Main Street built by A.J. Hayes on the east end of town. The home had been converted to a nursing home at some point in the 1960s, and in 1973; the owners were looking to sell the building and get out of debt. The West County Historical Association offered them $1,000 over what was owed and the owners accepted.

Some time after the Hazel Kibler Memorial Museum and Community House began operations, two gentlemen, Bob Pfiefer and Don Kuntz, representing the Elk Valley Model Railroading Club, approached the museum about renting the garage for their club space. The members moved in and have now become an integral part of the museum's operations.

By the late 1970s, Georgianna Read, failing in health, began setting up a trust fund to memorialize the family that had changed her life. Upon her death on May 1, 1982, her will announced that she was leaving the entire Battles Family Estate to be held in trust by the Trust Department of First National Bank of Pennsylvania and that she was naming the Erie County Historical Society the beneficiaries of the interest generated by that trust.

However, it would be almost nine years before the Erie County Historical Society would have free access to her house on Walnut Street to inventory its contents, having to progress through a series of legal battles to take possession of certain areas of the estate.

In 1984, several interested buyers approached the Girard School District in an attempt to purchase the Battles Memorial School, which had been vacant since 1981. The property was eventually sold to Kenneth Lochbaum who purchased the building for use as a full service physical therapy facility. After some remodeling and restoration, the business opened and operated until one fateful evening in 1992. A careless employee forgot to unplug a paraffin wax therapy spa, which overheated and ignited a fire that almost completely destroyed the building. Compounded by delays between the insurance carrier and the owner to settle the fire claim, the building stood open to the weather for almost two years. Once settlement occurred in the spring of 1994; the structure had so deteriorated that demolition was the only recourse. Fortunately, many artifacts were salvaged from the building. Some of them are now in the permanent collection of the Erie County Historical Society, the West County Historical Society, and the Girard School District. Two such artifacts are the stained glass window that resides over the library in the newly renovated Girard High School and the stone carved banner that proclaimed the name of the school, which will soon herald the entrance to the new high school sports complex.

In November of 1986, the Erie County Historical Society purchased the Battles Farmhouse from the Battles Trust along with 130 acres of land. After securing the property, they began restoration of the once grand family home. Under the watchful eye of the Girard community, the Erie County Historical Society carefully restored the very fabric of the house with the intentions of creating a museum to depict agricultural life in the Northwestern Pennsylvania Region.

In early 1987, the Erie County Historical Society purchased the R.S. Battles Bank building on Main Street, restored it, and with grand opening celebrations during the community's Dan Rice Days, allowed the community to view their accomplishments. The Battles Museums of Rural Life had been born, its mission defined as "to collect, preserve, study, and exhibit, the changes in rural life in Erie, Crawford, Mercer and Warren Counties as well as the adjacent areas of Chautauqua County, New York and Ashtabula County, Ohio from the year 1840 to the present as was reflected in the lives of the area's residents and their material culture."

In May of the same year, the Erie County Historical Society received as a gift the Universalist Unitarian Church, located on the southeast corner of Locust and Myrtle Streets from the congregation. Work immediately began on this project, beginning with the demolition of the attached Murray Social Hall, which had been previously condemned by health and safety officials. With the demolition complete, restoration efforts began and the building took on a dual purpose. For the Erie County Historical Society, it served as an orientation center for bus tours and school groups and as a facility to hold lectures and concerts. For the congregation, it remained their center of worship.

A little over a year later, the renovations and restorations were complete on the Battles Farmhouse. On a Sunday in October of 1988, the Erie County Historical Society once again opened its doors to the community to allow it to view their progress. In a four hour period, the newly restored building, now officially known as the R.S. Battles Farmhouse, received over 850 residents from the community as they strolled through the house and heard the plans for the future. The first floor would house a museum that through special exhibits would depict the agricultural lifestyle of those individuals who lived in Northwestern Pennsylvania and the surrounding region. The second floor would be used as staff living and office space. Trails were created in the woods and regularly scheduled ecological walks were conducted on the grounds. The farm's fields were once again under cultivation. It seemed that once again, the Battles Farm would be a prominent fixture in the landscape.

Chapter Ten

A NEW FOCUS ON HISTORY
1990-2003

By 1990 the population within Girard Borough had grown to 2,879 and to 4,772 within the township. The swelling in population brought with it a renewed interest in the community and its deep history. The Erie County Historical Society, having been successful in legal battles to obtain free access to the house at 306 Walnut Street, was inundated with community volunteers eager to lend a hand in the inventorying and cataloguing of the house's contents. Literally thousands of objects were recorded. Their location and description were written down to create a master inventory list of the objects that were once used by the Battles family. Two years and twenty 4-inch notebooks later, the initial inventory was completed and the organization once again began a major restoration project. The entire house was renovated and repaired; the existing foundations were reinforced and improved, the electrical and heating systems were upgraded and improved, and the plumbing system was brought up to code, along with numerous interior restorations to stabilize the house and its appearance.

A committee of 18 persons, consisting of professional tradesmen, architects, lawyers, businessmen, and other interested parties from both the Girard and Erie communities was formed and given the arduous task of making all the decisions with regards to the project. Susan Beates, the director of interpretation for the Erie County Historical Society at the time, was appointed the point staff person for the project. Living in North East, Pennsylvania at the time, most of her days and evenings were spent at Girard overseeing the contractors' and subcontractors' progress. It was her responsibility to insure that the work performed by the contractors conformed to both the wishes of the Battles Committee and the stipulations of Georgianna Read's will; which was not always an easy task. Read's will dictated the appearance of certain parts of the structure and the surrounding grounds in order to help preserve the site.

In a recent conservation, Susan Beates recalled how the committee agonized and debated over what type of roofing material to put on the building for almost 14 months. The material had to be in keeping with the historical integrity of the building, yet at the same time conform to Georgianna Read's will which stated that " . . . the house was to remain white with green shutters and a green roof."

Eventually, in 1992, the restoration phase of the project was completed and the building was officially dedicated as the Charlotte Elizabeth Battles Memorial Museum. Work immediately began on the interior interpretation of the house. It was decided by the Battles Museums Committee that the house should reflect the life of its principle owner, Charlotte Elizabeth Battles. The house should somehow convey to the visitor the personal spirit and convictions of its owner and yet, at the same time, conform to the museum's mission statement. Notwithstanding were the obstacles of modernization that had to be overcome or reversed in order to fit the historical timeline being portrayed. The committee finally agreed that the time frame would be 1952, the year that Miss Charlotte Elizabeth Battles passed away. In picking that date, the committee hoped to be able to tell her whole life story and at the same time show the house as it would have appeared in her final days.

In April of 1994, The Charlotte Elizabeth Battles Memorial Museum opened its doors to the Fairview Elementary third grade class. Regularly scheduled hours of operation were initiated and the Erie County Historical Society took a step back to view its accomplishments.

It was shortly thereafter that a simple event brought cohesiveness to the community like never before. For more than a century, the statue of "Shep" had stood vigilantly in the northeast section of the Girard Cemetery over the grave of H.C. Davis, who passed away in 1881. Local legend says that after his master's death, Shep refused to eat and upon his death was buried in the same plot, and the statue in his likeness was erected to memorialize the pet's devotion to this human companion. The actual story is far less romantic. Shep was poisoned in 1884 and was actually buried on the family's property in North Girard. Mrs. H.C. Davis commissioned the statue in 1889 and a photograph was used to sculpt the cast zinc figure of a life sized dog sitting in a captain's chair with its tail curled around its feet. The statue was placed to mark the family plot in the Girard Cemetery in 1890.

On September 30, 1993, the statue suddenly disappeared from the cemetery, the victim of an apparent theft. The Girard community was stunned and angered by the news. A reward fund was quickly organized; flyers bearing the photograph of the statue were distributed. Despite these efforts, local police were unable to come up with a solid lead for several years.

In 1997, Girard police received a phone call from an antique dealer in New Haven, Connecticut. The dealer had recently purchased a statue that matched the description of Girard's missing Shep. With the information obtained from the dealer, the police again began their investigation into the disappearance of the statue. The statue had apparently traveled through a succession of antique dealers in Pennsylvania, Ohio, New York, Maine, and Connecticut and was sold for anywhere from $6,000 to $20,000. The case was never solved as the police ran into another dead end, literally. The first buyers of the statue had passed away in 1995.

The Cosmopolite blared the following headline: "Hot Dog! Statue Stolen From Cemetery Is Found!" The Connecticut antique dealer was willing to return the statue and the community was instantly willing to foot the $800 bill to see Shep home. Once the statue arrived in Girard, the question of what to do with it remained. Due to the recent publicity, it was feared that if returned to its rightful place in the cemetery, it would surely quickly disappear. Numerous suggestions were forthcoming by the community members, but, in the end, the descendants of H.C. Davis, the rightful owners of the statue, donated the statue to the Borough of Girard. The statue was placed inside the Borough Building for all to see and remains there today.

A New Focus on History: 1990–2003

The business community of the 1990s was much different than the Main Street of today. Gone today is Marine Bank, Orr Jewelry, Brown Brothers Golden Dawn, Pennbank, Mighty Fine Donuts, The Lady Fair Shop, James Borland Real Estate, Simkovitce Tavern, Harpsts, Pearces County Florist, Sheer Elegance, Mid Town Tire Center, The Wood Loft, Lawson's Food and Deli, Colony Savings Bank, Siviks Pizza, Berman Bedding, Girard Hardware, For Art's Sake, Battery Barn, and Wauranne Tops and Bottoms; businesses that once lined our commercial district.

By 1995, the town's population had grown to 3,105 within the borough limits and to 5,153 within the township. Revitalization efforts on the part of the Borough Manager, Richard Higley; Borough Council, and the Girard–Lake City Chamber of Commerce were put into effect and a program to improve the façade of the business district was put into place. With matching funds available, many business owners took advantage of the opportunity to give their businesses a facelift. The program also helped install period street lamps, new trees, and a town clock.

The approaching new millennium brought with it yet another renewed focus on the town's history. The Erie County Historical Society, having just undergone a merger with the Erie Historical Museum & Planetarium, adopted a new master plan for developing the Battles Museums of Rural Life into a living history farm complex. The organization and the Battles Museums Committee realized that their hopes and dreams for the museum site were not materializing for a variety of reasons and that a change in direction was in order.

Hours of operation were changed from Tuesdays and Thursdays to Fridays, Saturdays, and Sundays. A staff, whose primary responsibility would be to work at the museum complex, was hired along with an ambitious new site administrator. Utilizing years of research, historical data, and the family artifacts, it was decided to incorporate living history into the R.S. Battles Farmhouse. Wearing period appropriate clothing, the museum staff would engage their visitors in conversation as they demonstrated appropriate activities for the year 1863. This concept, being successfully implemented in other parts of the country, seemed like a perfect fit for the struggling compound. Orchards were planted, heirloom vegetable gardens were established, and period outbuildings were erected, once again breathing life into Asa Battles Sr.'s farm.

Constantly on the cutting edge of the museum industry, the staff now proclaims their site to be interactive, a place where the visitor can participate in the day's activities. No longer does the visitor idly stand by and watch but is now an active participant in what takes place. Their efforts have well paid off! Where in prior years admission was very sparse, the museum hosted 7,198 visitors in 2002 and their excellent reputation is far reaching.

At the end of 2002, the Erie County Historical Society felt that the R.S. Battles Bank no longer met its current mission statement and sold the building to private owners with several conditions to preserve the historical integrity of the building. Today those owners have successfully preserved the historic fabric of the building as they have renovated it for adaptive reuse, housing retail space on the first floor and an apartment on the second floor.

In the early spring of 2003, historic animals returned to the R.S. Battles Farmstead for the first time in over 100 years in a continuation of the museum's development. As the farm raises only historic breeds of swine and chickens, not seen very often in today's society; the animals have once again taken up residence on the farm.

Girard, a small agricultural community founded in 1846, is now the largest township in Erie County and still has a strong farming presence that can be felt today. Its numerous farms within the limits contribute to the nation's annual agricultural product. The year end National Agricultural Statistics Service Agricultural Report for Erie County Pennsylvania, Girard Township for 2001 records the following information:

Crop Planted (1,000 acres)	Harvested (1,000 acres)	Yields in bushels per harvested acre
Corn	27.7	23.0	93.0
Oats	27.7	23.0	93.0

Soybeans	6.4	6.3	31.0
Wheat, All	2.0	1.8	48.0
Wheat, Winter	2.0	1.8	48.0

Girard has changed a lot since its incorporation in 1846. Many of the town's founding families, the Battleses, Websters, McConnells, Rices, and Harts, no longer reside in the tiny borough. Their only reminders to the community are the monuments and buildings that they have left behind. Most residents walk about town, appreciating the old buildings and the quaint lifestyle that the town affords them without ever understanding the hardships and self sacrifice that our founding families endured to place Girard on the map.

BIBLIOGRAPHY

Bates, Samuel P. *History of Erie County, Pennsylvania*. Chicago: Warner, Beers & Co., 1884.

Beers, F.W. *Atlas of Erie County Pennsylvania*. New York: Beers, Ellis & Soule, 1865.

Carlyon, David. *Dan Rice, The Most Famous Man You've Never Heard Of*. New York: Public Affairs, 2001.

Erie County Historical Society Archives and Collections, The Maynard Collection, Erie, PA.

Everts, Ensign, & Everts. *Combination Atlas Map of Erie County*. Philadelphia: Everts, Ensign, & Everts, 1876.

Freeman, Sabina Shields. *The Battles Story, The Life and Times of the Battles Family of Girard*. Fairview, PA: Sabina Shields Freeman, 1992.

"The History of Erie." WQLN Public Broadcasting of Northwestern Pennsylvania, 1976.

Kolb, Charles C. "The Erie Indians: Myth and Fact." *The Journal of Erie Studies* 10 (1986): 10–26.

Kunzog, John C. *The One-Horse Show, The Life and Times of Dan Rice, Circus Jester and Philanthropist*. Jamestown: John C. Kunzog, 1962.

Muller, Mary. *A Town At Presque Isle, A Short History of Erie, Pennsylvania to 1980*. Erie: The Erie County Historical Society, 1991.

Reed, John Elmer. *History of Erie County, Pennsylvania*. Topeka, Indianapolis: Historical Publishing Company, 1925.

"Remembering Erie." WQLN Public Broadcasting of Northwestern Pennsylvania, 1994.

Sanford, Laura G. *History of Erie County from its First Settlement*. New York: Laura G. Sanford, 1894.

A Souvenir of Erie, Penna. Illustrated. Erie: Herald Printing & Publishing, 1888.

"Unforgettable Erie." WQLN Public Broadcasting of Northwestern Pennsylvania, 1994.

Whitman, Benjamin. *History of Erie County, PA Illustrated, Part II*. Chicago: Warner, Beer & Co. 1884.

Wincik, Stephanie. *Ghosts of Erie County and Other Strange Tales*. Girard: Stephanie Wincik, 2002.

Wood, Russell and Claire. *A Collection of John Kelley's Articles Published in the Cosmopolite Herald from 1927 through 1941*. Girard: Russell and Claire Wood, 1991.

INDEX